RELIANT SPORTS CARS

DON PITHER

SUTTON PUBLISHING LIMITED

Sutton Publishing Limited
Phoenix Mill · Thrupp · Stroud
Gloucestershire · GL5 2BU

First published 2000

Title page photograph: the sword emblem
representing the Scimitar was used in
various forms on different models, both on
the external bodywork as well as the
steering-wheel boss.

British Library Cataloguing in Publication Data
A catalogue record for this book is available from the
British Library.

ISBN 0-7509-2388-1

Typeset in 10.5/13.5 Photina.
Typesetting and origination by
Sutton Publishing Limited.
Printed in Great Britain by
Cromwell Press, Trowbridge, Wiltshire.

ACKNOWLEDGEMENTS

I would like to express my appreciation for the considerable help and support I have
received from many people, including Ken Britton, Steve Cropley, Pam and Geoff
Eldridge, Alison Flowers, Olwen Greany, Rupert Harding, Fred Quigley, David Page,
Margaret Pither, Tony Stevens, Michael Ware, Ray Wiggin, and members of Reliant
Sabre and Scimitar Owners Club.

Ray Wiggin, Managing Director of Reliant from 1964 to 1977, was effectively the 'Father of
Reliant Sports Cars' and is seen here looking suitably proud of the range of Reliant products in
1967 ranging from three-wheeled Regals to the latest Scimitar Coupés.

CONTENTS

FOREWORD

Reliant was a 'one product – one market' company when I joined the Tamworth firm in February 1959. The 'one product' was a glass-fibre-bodied three-wheeled passenger car with a van derivative and the 'one market' was the UK. Production was running at about thirty-five vehicles a week.

Even at that time two of Reliant's young designers, David Page and Ron Heathcote, and the Sales Director, Tom Scott, had ideas about developing a small sports car one day and running the manufacture of it alongside the traditional Reliant three-wheeler. However, first of all it was decided that a new all-aluminium engine and gearbox needed to be designed to replace the 1930s design that was still being used at that time. It was envisaged that these units would be used on the three-wheelers initially and later a high-performance version could power a small sports car. Thus the seeds of a sporting car for Reliant were sown very early. However, initiatives outside the company eventually changed these priorities and the actual train of events became very different from those envisaged in the early days.

As you will read in the following chapters, the initiatives came from the Managing Director of Autocars Limited of Haifa, Israel, Mr Itzhak Shubinsky, who wanted to develop an export market in the USA to help the Israeli economy and to further expand his business. The problem was, however, that Mr Shubinsky was always a man in a great hurry and he didn't want to wait for two or three years for a normal design/development/production programme to be completed; he wanted the product in the market in twelve months.

The solution Mr Shubinsky was looking for arose out of a visit to the London Racing Car Show in January 1960. There he saw as exhibits on their respective stands a relatively simple-to-make chassis designed by LMB Components and an attractive glass-fibre sports-car body exhibited by Ashley Associates. He then visited Reliant in Tamworth and said, 'There you are. Put the two together for me and we can have a new car ready for production in no time!' In fact it didn't work out at all like that, but even so this concept set Reliant on a course of developing its own sports car and the first vehicle left the Tamworth factory bound for New York in March 1961.

As far as Tamworth is concerned the first sports car produced at Reliant was the Sabra – a name applied to a native of Israel – and it was destined for the USA market. The car was originally intended to be produced in Haifa (which it was – later) but 'our man in a hurry' wanted cars in the USA market more quickly than would have been possible if he had had to wait until the Israeli-produced cars were available. Therefore, Reliant took the view that if it had to make cars for the USA then why not Anglicise the model, call it 'Sabre' and launch it in the UK market. And that is what happened.

The Sabre sold, but ever so slowly, and much heart-searching took place in the Reliant board room as to how to sell more cars through the network of dealers that was being established. It was recognised that two major improvements were needed – increased power was required and a more pleasing body shape was needed. As a result the more powerful Sabre 6 was introduced in October 1963, and a new body was commissioned from David Ogle Ltd of Letchworth. That company, under the leadership of Tom Karen, produced the very graceful Scimitar GT which went into production in 1964.

The Scimitar GT sold reasonably well but Reliant was looking for a solution to satisfy a perceived demand for a design of sports saloon that could provide reasonable accommodation for four people as well as lots of luggage. Several attempts at designing such a vehicle resulted in a model that looked more like a GT version of a funeral hearse – and ended up in the waste paper bin.

Market surveys taken at this time indicated that Reliant's plans were appropriate. The results showed that there was a potential market of 40,500/50,000 a year for such a car and even allowing for the fact that Reliant might clinch less than 10 per cent of the potential sales it would have been big business for the Tamworth firm. The work on a suitable design continued until Tom Karen asked me to look at a full-sized paper and cardboard mock-up that he had produced in his model shop at Letchworth. So I went along one October evening in 1967. It was a brilliant design and my comment was quick and to the point: 'That's it! Go ahead! Let's have a prototype by Easter!' That car became the Scimitar GTE and not only sold very well for Reliant but set a fashion in car design that is traceable in almost every model in the market today, twenty-two years later. Well done Ogle!

The success of the GTE further consolidated Reliant's thinking about its place in the British motor industry. By 1977 the Reliant Forward Model Policy contained a range of sporting models which included, a GTE replacement, a replacement for the Turkish-made saloon (Anadol), an open two-door GT, a five-door executive performance saloon, and a small two-seater sports car. It was planned that these models would be in production by the end of the fourth year of a seven-year programme. Other changes were to include forming a separate company, Scimitar Cars Limited, to handle the sporting four-wheelers while Reliant would continue to take care of the vitally important three-wheeler business, which at its peak sold over 13,000 vehicles a year.

However, these plans were not to be fulfilled. Reliant Motor Group Limited had been owned by the Hodge Group of Cardiff since 1962 but suddenly found itself a subsidiary of Standard Chartered Bank Limited after that company took over the Hodge Group in 1976. In 1977 Reliant was purchased by John Nash of John Nash Industries, Kettering, and the policy changed from 'expansionist' to 'contractionist'. It must be said that times were difficult and immediate prospects were very poor. Understandably, Mr Nash wanted a free hand and the result was that we parted company in a very civilised way at the end of 1977.

That is the background to Reliant's foray into the sports-car world, which continued for a further decade, as you will read in the following pages. I am sure you will enjoy Don Pither's book – and I wish it well.

Ray Wiggin
Lichfield
November 1999

5

INTRODUCTION

The title of this volume begs three questions. Firstly what is a sport car? Who are Reliant? How did they become involved in sports cars?

The first query is probably the hardest to answer since there is no positive definition of a sports car, though most enthusiasts would agree that such a vehicle must have only two doors, two primary seats, and the performance, handling and styling must emphasise sporting rather than functional characteristics. The requirement for a drop-head as opposed to a fixed-head bodywork should not necessarily be the determining factor as many traditional two-seaters are available in both guises. Equally, a drop-head four-seater is not perforce a sporting car.

Most sports-car makers have arisen from the inspiration of an enthusiastic engineer who first built a special for his own use and then found that a small business evolved by virtue of requests for replicas from colleagues or fellow competitors. Jaguar, Lotus and Marcos are successful examples of this process, whose originators were William Lyons, Colin Chapman and Jem Marsh respectively. Alternatively, other marques have emerged as a sporting branch of a larger mass-production manufacturer of which MG is perhaps the best example, which stemmed from the Morris range of the Nuffield Group. Reliant sports cars, however, were the result of a request by one of its customers, Autocars of Israel, who were interested in branching out in the USA market. Reliant are best known for their three-wheeled range of vehicles, which date back to 1933 when Tom Williams designed a three-wheeled van based on the front forks and handlebars of a Triumph motor cycle, linked to a live rear axle driven by a motor-cycle engine. Williams was working for Raleigh in Nottingham at the time and was instrumental in building the Raleigh Safety Seven, based on his own project, of which 3,000 were sold in 3 years. He left Raleigh in 1934 to start his own company, Reliant Engineering. His first model, a three-wheeled van, was licensed on 1 January 1935. Tom continued to develop his designs and soon adopted the 747cc Austin 7 alloy engine as a power source in 1938. At the start of the Second World War Reliant built their own alloy side-valve engine based on the Austin unit. This was an early example of Reliant's self-sufficiency and they have continued to build their own small car engines, albeit in OHV form after 1963, to this day.

In 1956 Reliant built their first car with a body made from glass-reinforced polyester resin, more commonly known today as fibreglass or GRP for short. In the mid-1950s the kit-car industry was born out of a desire to produce exciting home-built cars in the lean post-war years when sports cars were rare and expensive. These were usually based on propriety saloon cars, of which the Austin 7 and Ford 8 were favourites, and fitted with fibreglass sports bodywork. It was from just such a body design that the Reliant sports car developed.

Up to this point in its production history Reliant had lived up to its name by being almost entirely self-reliant in the components used in its vehicles. All the bodywork moulding and chassis construction was done in-house as well as the construction of engines, gearboxes, rear axles, suspension and steering parts. Virtually the only bought-in items were glass, electrical and braking components, carburettors and certain trim items such as door handles and steering wheels.

In the late 1950s, Reliant designed and built a four-wheeled estate car called the Sussita for Autocars of Haifa as a result of the intense interest in Israel of the newly appointed Assistant General Manager Ray Wiggin. The Sussita and its saloon counterpart, the Carmel, were produced in knock-down form for assembly and sale in Israel only. Following the success of this venture Autocars were looking to export suitable cars to the largely sympathetic and lucrative American market. However, the current models were hardly appropriate and the Americans were hungry for small sports cars of the type not produced in the USA, as was evident by their appetite for MGs and Triumphs. In pursuit of this idea, Mr Shubinsky, the Managing Director of Autocars, visited the 1960 Racing Car Show and was attracted to the Ashley fibreglass bodyshell exhibited there, for fitting to Austin 7 or Ford 8 chassis. Such bases were not suitable for the American market but a chassis designed by Les Ballamy, exhibited on another stand, did seem to fit the bill as a basis for the Ashley body. As a result, a deal was arranged for Autocars to use the Ashley body design suitably modified to fit the Ballamy chassis, which had been intended as the basis of the EB Debonair car also exhibited on the stand. Thus the Ashley moulds and Ballamy suspension components were purchased as well so that initial production could start in a short period of time. Autocars had no hesitation in commissioning Reliant to mould the bodyshells for their new sports-car project as well as build the initial supply of chassis for export to Israel along the lines of the Sussita and Carmel. So the Sabra sports car was born, and as we shall see, the whole range of Reliant sports cars evolved through this arrangement with Autocars.

Ray Wiggin was also attracted to the project and felt there must be a market in the UK for such a car. When Autocars ran into financial difficulties and the Sabra future looked uncertain Reliant were naturally keen to make use of the development work they had put into this joint venture. Thus at the 1961 Motor Show at Earls Court in October a right-hand-drive version of the new car, with the name Sabre, was exhibited for the UK market after an amazingly short gestation period of just eighteen months.

The new car was initially powered by the Ford Consul four-cylinder 1703cc engine producing 57bhp, mated to a delightful ZF four-speed gearbox and was eventually called the Sabre 4. While its performance was reasonably competitive, its price, handling and build quality were not and only fifty-five cars were sold over the two years it was in production. This lethargic start did not deter Ray Wiggin who even authorised entering works cars in international rallies to promote sales. He decided that giving the car more power from the Ford Zodiac six-cylinder engine and modifying the front bodywork as well as introducing an attractive fixed-head design would improve the chances of Reliant selling many more cars. Even though further forays into international rallying, with some class wins, were undertaken, the competition was too strong and established and only seventy-seven cars left the Tamworth factory between 1963 and 1965.

Perhaps it was Bill Boddy's comment in *Motor Sport* that 'Reliant would have a very good product if they started with a clean sheet of paper' that prompted Ray Wiggin to search hard for a more elegant bodyshape as a means of attracting more customers. At the 1962 Motor Show, Reliant found a solution to their problem in the shape of an Ogle-bodied Daimler SX250, commissioned by a cosmetic company executive. Fortunately for Reliant, the Daimler project foundered after two cars had been made on the SP250 chassis. Ogle were understandably keen to capitalise on their efforts and measurements soon revealed that their elegant 2+2 coupé body would fit the Sabre 6 chassis with minimal alteration, at least externally. Again, almost by accident, a new model, the Scimitar, was conceived. The new business relationship between Reliant and Ogle was to be both long-lived and mutually very successful, only terminating when Ray Wiggin left Reliant following the Nash family's acquisition of Reliant in 1977.

Fortuitously for Reliant, Ogle chose the new Scimitar as a basis for a glass-roofed project commissioned by Triplex to demonstrate tinted and heated laminated glass in automotive applications. This lead to the first royal connection with Reliant when the Duke of Edinburgh used this unique car for a couple of years. Perhaps even more significantly this particular design inspired the concept of a sporting estate car model which emerged three years later as the revolutionary Scimitar GTE exhibited at the 1968 Motor Show.

The original Scimitar Coupé model used the same straight-six Ford engine as the Sabre 6 with the addition of three SU carburettors, but when Ford dropped this engine in favour of the 3 litre V6 design in 1967, Reliant were obliged to follow suit. Thus the GTE model commenced production powered by the V6 engine alongside the Coupé version for a couple of years. Just over 1,000 of the Coupés were produced before production capacity and sales figures spelled the end of the Coupé in 1970. The motoring press greeted the GTE with much deserved acclaim and Reliant production capacity was stretched to the point where a new factory on the other side of the A5 in Tamworth was built, largely due to the inspiration of Ray Wiggin who was by now Reliant's Managing Director. A further boost to the popularity of the new car was provided when Princess Anne was given a GTE by her parents for her birthday in 1970. Ever since she has been a loyal fan, owning eight successive versions.

In 1975, when sales were still buoyant, Reliant chose to revamp the GTE by making it larger with a more luxurious interior and a specification that included much-needed power steering. The SE6 model was now aimed more at the executive market than the sporting division and ran into competition with Rover and BMW products, but the teething troubles and build quality experienced with the SE6 mitigated against its continued rate of success with this critical clientele. However, quality did gradually improve and sales were maintained reasonably well until the recession of 1980, which happened to coincide with the change of engine, again dictated by Ford, to the 2.8 Cologne-built V6. Simultaneously, Reliant introduced a convertible GTC model, the last design to be accepted by Reliant from Ogle. This model should have been a great success after the demise of the troublesome Triumph Stag, but economic circumstances caused stockpiles of GTE and GTC models to build up, to such an extent that production was temporarily halted and only restarted again on a much reduced scale in 1983. It finally ceased at Tamworth in 1986. This was not quite the end of the GTE, however, as a Japanese-financed company, Middlebridge, acquired the rights and machinery to continue production in a purpose-built factory in Nottingham. This proved to be rather ambitious as the car was now very dated in specification, although the body shape was still outstanding. The accompanying price increase coupled with financial mismanagement led to the auction of the remaining stock in 1990 after just seventy-seven Middlebridge Scimitars had been completed.

The lack of development of the GTE undoubtedly contributed to its demise, particularly as the new Nash management in 1977 decided to pursue the small sports-car market once more. This was a sensible move in many ways as British sports cars had virtually all but disappeared with the exception of Morgan and a few small specialists. Unfortunately, Reliant spurned the design suggestion of Tony Stevens, using their small car running gear as a basis, in favour of a controversial Michelotti design incorporating a brand-new chassis. Furthermore, Reliant contracted out the body and chassis production to companies in the UK and Germany when they were easily capable of producing such items themselves. Sadly, the design was not a happy one and the assembly was very costly which led to poor sales and a succession of collapses of the company. Production of all Scimitars finally staggered to a halt in 1996 and the company is now only producing three-wheelers, which have been a stable product throughout the history of Reliant.

THE SPORTS CAR RANGE

1960	Sabra Special	Prototype CBF 941
1961	SE1	Sabre 4 two-seater sports and Coupé (208 produced)
1962	SE2	Sabre 6 GT Coupé (77 produced)
1963	SE3	V8-engined GT car – abandoned
1964	SE4	Straight-six Scimitar Coupé (297 produced)
1966	SE4a/b	3 litre V6 Scimitar Coupé (591 produced)
1967	SE4c	2.5 litre V6 Scimitar Coupé (118 produced)
1968	SE5	Scimitar GTE 3 litre (4,311 produced)
1971	SE5a	Uprated SE5 (5,105 produced)
1975	SE6	Enlarged GTE 3 litre (543 produced)
1976	SE6a	Improved SE6 (3,877 produced)
1977	SE7	Four-door version of the SE6 – abandoned
1978	SE8	GTC 3 litre prototype KJW 247T
1979	SE6b	2.8 litre SE6 GTE (437 produced)
1980	SE8b	2.8 litre GTC convertible (442 produced)
1982	SE82	Bertone-bodied V8 GTE replacement – prototype only
1984	SS1	Michelotti-designed two-seater, 1300cc and 1600cc (about 1,000 produced)
1986	1800ti	Nissan turbo-engined version of SS1 (about 500 produced)
1990	SST	Modified GRP bodywork 1400cc, 1600cc and 1800cc models
1991	Sabre	Further bodywork modification
1994	Sabre	Rover 1.4 and 2 litre engines introduced
1995	Sabre	Production ceased in May (about 200 Sabres produced)

CHAPTER ONE

THE SABRES

CBF 941 was the first attempt by Reliant to produce a sports car and as such is fortunate to have survived. Many such prototypes were butchered by the makers in attempts to improve them before finally being cut up and discarded. This example was lucky enough to be acquired by ex-Reliant employees when the company had finished with it. Fortunately, it was restored in the 1980s after passing through many owners' hands and since then has been circulated through classic car dealers in an attempt to find a sympathetic and appreciative owner. Finished in pale blue, it really is a most attractive little car and has recently found a good home.

The car industry in Britain during the 1950s was still concentrating as much as possible on satisfying the demand for exporting large percentages of their production to rebuild British currency reserves depleted during the Second World War. The USA was the UK's biggest market then and being more affluent their taste was for the British sports car following the successful launch of the MG-T series. The home market was also hungry for cars, but for those of a more practical nature. The luxury of a sports car was confined to higher income brackets only.

This situation led to the creation of a small industry composed of enthusiastic engineers who offered kits to convert basic, cheap saloons into attractive sporting cars by virtue of the revolutionary material known as glass-reinforced polyester resin (GRP), which was capable of being moulded into any shape forming a strong, smooth and rust-proof structure. The quality of these early mouldings did not compare with conventional steel pressings widely used in mass production, but the exciting styling possible for modest expense was more than enough compensation. The whole concept was also made possible because most cars were still based on separate chassis construction, so replacing the bodywork was relatively easy for the home mechanic for whom the kits were intended. The most common 'donor' cars of this era were the pre-war Austin 7 and Ford 8 saloons which by the 1950s were past their best and only fit for scrapping in many cases. Thus an increasing range of kit cars were spawned, costing only a few hundred pounds to construct, whereas the cheapest production sports car cost in the region of £700 to £800, if you could obtain one at all.

The more professional kits began to appear at specialist motor shows such as the Racing Car Show, and it was here in 1960 that the story of Reliant sports cars really started. Reliant themselves were not exhibiting as they were specialist manufacturers of three-wheeled economy cars, albeit with bodies made of GRP. However, one of the prominent specialist body makers, Ashley, was present with some very neat drop-head and closed bodies suitable for fitting to Austin 7 or Ford 1172cc chassis. It was the Ashley stand that caught the attention of Mr Shubinsky of Autocars from Haifa in Israel. Autocars already produced fibreglass-bodied saloons and estate cars in Israel from body moulds developed by Reliant following an arrangement negotiated by Ray Wiggin. It occurred to Shubinsky that in the Ashley there was the prospect of producing an attractive sports car themselves, for export to the USA, based on this ready made design, of impressive quality for the period. They had the facilities to produce such a body already in place but did not as yet have a suitable basic chassis on which to mount a sports type body. Coincidentally, the chassis from a totally different concern, designed by L. Ballamy, was also on show under the same roof and swift measurement revealed that this would fit the Ashley body. This was not an improbable situation because most manufacturers catered for the Ford 1172cc chassis and many of the components and measurements from the Ballamy chassis came from Ford sources.

Within nine months Reliant had made the necessary modifications to both chassis and body so that they mated satisfactorily, while some improvements were made to the Ballamy leaf-spring suspension by employing coil spring and damper units instead. However, the need to use the original linkages, as part of the deal negotiated by Autocars, restricted any radical developments. The front bodywork was also modified to include large chrome overriders as protection for American owners from parking assaults. Autocars chose the name Sabra for the new car, after an Israeli cactus that was featured in their badge.

Autocars intended to construct the Sabra in Haifa from kits of mechanical parts sent from Reliant in Tamworth and mould the bodies locally. However, in order to speed up the process Reliant built 208 of the cars, of which about 140 were exported direct to the USA on behalf of the Israeli firm, while the rest went to Europe. Reliant eventually sent about 50 kits to Autocars, from which they assembled about 45 cars between 1961 and 1965 and of these about 20 are known today worldwide. About 36 of the UK-built Sabras still exist. Autocars went into liquidation in 1971, which ended Reliant's relationship with the Israeli market, and the remaining kits were auctioned some years later.

Following the introduction of the Sabra, Reliant realised that there might also be a home market for such a two-seater, requiring very little alteration from the Sabra already made. Thus the Reliant stand at the 1961 Motor Show featured a right-hand-drive version called the Sabre as their first purpose-built sports car. Although the 1703cc Ford Consul engine provided adequate performance in its class, the handling, appearance and price of the finished product was less than appealing with the result that only fifty-five were made. The following road test figures from *Autocar* magazine illustrate clearly how uncompetitive the Sabre 4 was compared with the contemporary sports cars such as the 1600cc Sunbeam Alpine and the 1600cc MGA in terms of price and performance:

	Price (£)	Max. Speed (mph)	0–60mph (secs)	50–70mph in top gear (secs)	mpg
Sabre 4	1,128	90.1	16.6	14.1	28.8
Alpine	971	98.4	14.0	11.7	25.5
MGA	940	100.9	14.2	11.9	24.1

In order to address the problem of competing more favourably with mass-production sports cars, Ray Wiggin decided to introduce a six-cylinder version of the Sabre using the current Ford Zodiac 2553cc engine. With the revision of the frontal appearance by removing the front overhang and the overriders in favour of a broad grille and moulded-in bumpers to match those at the rear, he hoped that the Sabre 6 or SE2 would now attract more customers. Further changes to the front suspension were made after seventeen cars had been produced by incorporating a double wishbone system utilising many Triumph TR4 parts. Reliant continued their rallying programme, as we shall see in the next chapter, in order to promote the marque, and a great deal was learned from this exercise.

However, sales still did not take off as hoped and perhaps one of the reasons for this was the absence of an open drop-head version, even though one was displayed at the 1963 Motor Show. It seems that only two such cars were ever completed and perhaps this was a mistake as most of the competition were open cars with the option of a hard-top. As far as figures were concerned, the Sabre 6 was now far more competitive than its predecessor, as the table below, sourced from *Autocar* road tests, shows:

	Price (£)	Max. Speed (mph)	0–60mph (secs)	50–70mph in top gear (secs)	mpg
Sabre 6	1,075	110.5	12.2	9.1	20.3
Healey 3000	1,190	117.0	10.4	7.1	17.1
Triumph TR4	1,032	102.5	10.9	9.4	22.5

Despite all the improvements and rallying exploits only seventy-seven cars were actually made, mostly equipped with a Ford overdrive gearbox to enhance high-speed refinement, and only the last model produced was fitted with the ZF unit.

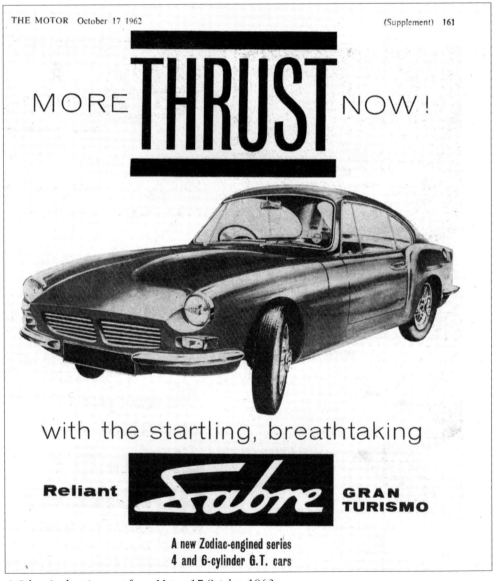

A Sabre 6 advertisement from *Motor*, 17 October 1962.

The Ashley GT bodyshell mounted on a Ford Popular chassis which attracted Mr Shubinsky's attention at the 1960 Racing Car Show. It was also available in open two-seater form and eventually formed the basis of the Sabra sports car commissioned by Autocars of Israel, who purchased the rights to use this bodyshell and moulds for production purposes. Modifications were made to the flip-up front section by designers from Reliant who were contracted to build kits for Autocars to assemble in Haifa.

The rolling chassis of the EB Debonair kit car also exhibited at the same 1960 show as the Ashley. This chassis was designed by Leslie Ballamy of LMB Components of Guildford. It featured a development of the conventional swing-axle front suspension of which Ballamy was a leading devotee, having assisted Allards with their swing-axle-equipped sports cars. In this latest application the swinging arm locating the front wheels is inclined at an angle of 15° to the line of the chassis, to reduce camber change during bump and rebound while retaining the original transverse leaf spring from the Ford chassis both at the front and rear, albeit with additional radius arms to help locate the rear axle instead of Ford's torque tube method.

The prototype built by Reliant as a result of the arrangement made by Autocars of Israel to purchase the rights for the Ashley bodyshell and EB chassis, from which this unique car is derived. At this stage the bodywork was virtually unaltered but the front and rear sidelights were changed to utilise units already fitted to the Reliant economy range of cars. The suspension had already been modified to employ coil-spring/shock-absorber units with twin trailing arms and panhard rod locating the rear axle in place of the transverse leaf springs used by the EB chassis. Originally, this car was left-hand drive, but subsequent owners have converted it to right-hand drive as it never left the UK. The engine was from the Ford Consul together with the Ford gearbox, but the latter was subsequently replaced by the close-ratio ZF unit on production cars.

Eddie Pepall of Reliant drew up possible re-designs for the Ashley body to give it a sharper appearance incorporating prominent front overriders in place of bumpers to cater for the American market. Apart from this modified front end, the rest of the open version of the eventual Sabra followed the Ashley lines very closely enabling Reliant to utilise the Ashley moulds purchased by Autocars. Reliant were chosen for this contract because of their previous and on-going production of saloon and estate cars with fibreglass bodies for Autocars, known as the Carmel and Sussita.

The chassis for the Sabra was totally redesigned by David Page of Reliant for Autocars. The only restriction, apart from being able to support the Ashley bodyshell, was that the front and rear suspension arms had to be retained from the Ballamy design as large numbers of these had been purchased by Autocars when they made the deal with EB components. Page chose to use coil-spring damper units but the watt linkage on the rear axle imposed a twisting action on the axle during roll, and the transverse location was achieved by angling these radius arms outwards.

The completed Sabra followed Pepall's design very closely and the rather controversial front horn-like overriders appear to be body coloured in this early example. However, the standard of fibreglass moulding was excellent for this period as Reliant probably had more experience of this method of producing car bodywork than any other company in the world. The moulding around the headlights seems to indicate the possible fitment of clear plastic covers to follow the wing line and add to streamlining when the car was in production.

The hinging forward bonnet seen here allowed unrivalled access to the engine and front suspension and all ancillaries such as the windscreen-wiper motor prominently situated behind the right-hand front wheel arch. This construction permitted quicker and thus cheaper servicing and component replacement, particularly the engine, as well as simpler repair after front-end collisions. Note the fitting of Ace wheel embellishers to the standard steel wheels. Wire wheels were naturally a popular option.

This rear view illustrates the use of a moulded-in rear bumper, which was eventually covered with chromed metal sections to imply they were separate components. The rear light units were 'borrowed' from the contemporary Alfa Romeo Guilietta Sprint, which seemed an expensive choice at the time and certainly is now when they need replacing. The shallowness of the rear boot is apparent here, and remember it also had to house the spare wheel since the fuel tank was beneath this compartment.

All the Sabras were naturally left-hand drive for the US market and the Cactus badge can be clearly seen at the centre of the wood-rimmed Les Leston steering wheel. The seven-dial instrumentation was very comprehensive although the prominent location of the clock is strange for a sports car when a combined temperature and oil gauge might have been more suitable in this position. The Sabra featured one of the first examples of a completely moulded dashboard assembly in any production car, which is virtually universal now. Also, very handily placed is the dainty gear lever controlling the delightful ZF four-speed gearbox, which was another expensive component and only fitted to Osca and Lotus Elite cars.

The Sabra at the 1961 New York Motor Show. The car is alongside the Carmel saloon and the Sussita estate cars, also produced in knock-down kit form by Reliant. Initially, Reliant built 208 complete cars at Tamworth for direct export to the USA and some 50 kits were then sent to Autocars in Israel. However, Autocars went bankrupt before many of these were completed, and the local customs impounded several of these kits exported from England and the contents were later auctioned off in the 1970s providing some UK dealers with desirable ZF gearboxes, much sought after by Lotus Elite owners.

Reliant also exhibited their Anglicised version of the Sabra, known as the Sabre, at the 1961 London Motor Show. As a result of Autocars' financial difficulties and the inviting home market, Reliant decided to justify their investment by producing a version of the Sabra for Britain which only involved converting the steering, dashboard and controls to right-hand drive. The reception this received was rather mixed due to the unusual frontal appearance and the peculiar geometry of the front and rear suspensions imposed on Reliant at the outset.

7947 WD was a sister car to the model on the following page, also having a Sabra chassis number, but fitted with an optional, quite handsome and well-made hard-top, which is very much sought after these days. The slotted steel wheels seen here are fitted with simple chrome hubcaps, although the Ace rim embellishers seen on the Sabra were often used on the British cars too. This particular car was used privately for circuit racing after being sold by the factory and now resides, together with 7946 WD, in the Valler household in Sussex.

Towards the end of Sabra production a fixed-head version was introduced following Eddie Pepall's original drawing. This blended very well with the rear wing line but the square rear wheel arches and front 'horns' still looked unhappy and no doubt contributed to the lukewarm reception the car received in the USA against the competing MGs and Triumphs being imported at the same time. The Sabra did have wind-up windows in both open and closed versions, and this was not universal in sports cars of that era.

7946 WD was one of the first examples of the Sabre, although it has in fact got a Sabra chassis number so was clearly intended for export but was converted by Reliant as a development car for the home market. There were no external body alterations made at this stage but the perspex lamp

covers never seemed to feature on UK cars. This particular car was rescued in the 1970s by the late Roger Valler, who found it in Scotland with the chassis cut in half, a state in which it still exists.

This stylised publicity photograph of the new Sabre illustrates a modified round wheel arch that suits the car so much better. The chrome front overriders and absence of fared-in headlamps still prevent the car from being balanced and handsome in most people's eyes. It also restricted the appeal of the car in the UK so that a total of only fifty-five were made and sold during the model's two-year production life between 1961 and 1963.

A final version of the Sabra GT Coupé addressed some of the criticisms by re-shaping the rear wheel arches with a round profile that matched the front ones and at the same time added a slight flaring which created a more solid appearance. The headlamps were now covered with perspex cowls, but the overriders, necessary for the US market, still spoiled the frontal appearance. This was only remedied later with the introduction of the six-cylinder stable mate, which had a revised front moulding that incorporated conventional bumpers.

One of the first six-cylinder Sabres was in drop-head form, seen here. Still retaining the same rear-light assemblies as the Sabre 4, as well as the semi-swing axle front suspension, it had a shorter front nose section. Ironically, only one other Sabre 6 drop-head was ever made, later in 1963 and exhibited at Earl's Court the same year, and that had rounded rear wheel arches and A40-style rear lights and wishbone front suspension.

The body moulding shop at Reliant's Kettlebrook site. This photograph shows the large percentage of women employed in this department, rather surprising considering the potentially dangerous materials used in the fibreglass process. No doubt the care put into this operation contributed to the high-quality mouldings produced by Reliant, which enabled the company to secure contracts to produce these mouldings for other industrial applications, such as Ford truck cabs. The bodies seen being made are for the three-wheeler range but the process was similar for the Sabra and Sabre bodies.

Sabras and Sabres being assembled in the same building on a very compact hand-operated production line with individual job stations. It is interesting to see drop-head and fixed-head versions being produced consecutively and even a three-wheeler has crept into the top right-hand corner of the shop, possibly for some form of rectification rather than assembly. A rare hard-top can be seen casually balanced on the storage shelves on the right of the picture.

The advantage of fibreglass body construction is that quite dramatic changes can be made quickly and relatively cheaply. Thus Reliant were able to address the adverse reaction to the Sabre's bonnet shape without interrupting production by just re-jigging the bonnet assembly with a more conventional broad grille without moving the headlamp positions. At the same time quarter bumper mouldings were built in to match the rear bumper and small overriders, 'borrowed' from the E-type Jaguar, gave an attractive finishing touch to the design. 187 DWD, seen here, started life in 'long-nose' form and while in Reliant's possession was fitted with this later bonnet. The process of retro-fitting the later assembly was subsequently carried out by other owners, particularly if replacement was necessary due to accidental damage.

This profile shot of the short-nose conformation proves how much better balanced the car now looks, leaving only the square rear wheel arches to offend the eye. Note the use of chrome metal bumper coverings and the improved shut-lines of the bodywork, which illustrates the quality of the Reliant moulds and preparation. 187 DWD has been frequently used in historic rallies in Ireland, where it still resides.

Two Sabres used in competition being fettled in the area of the twin SU carburettors in the workshop of Argyle Motors. The tubular exhaust manifolds and front anti-roll bars are not standard and the fitting of clear headlamp covers and the removal of the front overriders are further indications of their participation in club racing. Argyle Motors were very active in preparing Sabres for competition and there was a local race track at Aintree.

Perhaps this is some celebrity taking delivery of a new Sabre at a dealer's showroom with the approval of her poodle. The Reliant Engineering label on the ignition key denotes that it is a new car and although it might be a publicity stunt a number of stars from the entertainment world did buy Sabres as they had something of a glamorous image. In common with some other open sports cars you can see the bracing strut at the centre of the windscreen behind the rear-view mirror. The mere 112 miles on the clock is likely to be the delivery and demonstration mileage from Tamworth.

The four-cylinder Sabre had not been a sales success, although it did not disgrace itself in rallying and club racing. Ray Wiggin decided that upgrading this relatively expensive car to six-cylinder power might be the way to achieve more sales. Eddie Pepall again produced drawings, one of which is seen here, for the closed coupé version of the proposed car. Although very similar to the short-nosed Sabre 4, as it retrospectively became known, there were subtle differences to the rear wing line and wheel arches while the previously revised front end was not altered drastically.

The publicity car seen here shows how faithfully Reliant pattern makers were to the Pepall proposal which resulted in a most elegant sports car at last. The bonnet bulge was introduced to clear the longer six-cylinder engine while the flared wheel arches accommodated a wider rear axle and different front track. The wire wheels suit the car perfectly and the optional spotlights enhance its sporting flavour. This car is presently being restored in Holland.

The rear three-quarter view of the Sabre 6 is possibly its best aspect and the rear light units 'borrowed' from the A40 Farina blend well with the raised rear-wing profile. After seventeen cars were produced the front suspension was very wisely altered from the early semi-swing axle design to a double wishbone layout from the Triumph TR4. *Autocar*, when testing this car, reported that, 'the handling is excellent and completely predictable . . . on twisting main roads its almost neutral (rack and pinion) steering allows it to be really hustled round the corners, a very slight oversteer setting in when the limit is reached'.

A Sabre 6 rolling chassis was on the Reliant stand at the 1963 Motor Show and being an early example still had the Ballamy designed semi-swing axle front suspension and Ford's floor manual gear change, later redesigned by Reliant. The Zodiac single carburettor engine with twin exhaust

system is clearly evident as is the overdrive unit on the back of the gearbox. Pirelli Cinturato tyres were very highly rated in the 1960s and were fitted as standard to all Sabres.

249 JNX was the car submitted by Reliant to *Autocar* magazine for road test and was given a far better reception than its predecessor. Performance was naturally better showing a top speed of just over 110mph on average with the magazine commenting that, 'the Sabre Six can get from A to B very quickly without resorting to particularly energetic driving'. The replacement Ford Zodiac overdrive gearbox proved rather clumsy after the splendid close-ratio ZF unit fitted to the Sabre 4, but the spread of ratios suited the car better. *Autocar* praised the driving position and visibility as well as the true grand touring nature of the car.

The moulded dashboard was little altered for the Sabre 6 but the optional radio is seen here. Also the gear lever is much higher on the car now that a Ford unit is fitted and was closer to hand than the ZF one. The overdrive handle can just be seen behind the gear lever and when engaged would automatically change up to overdrive after the accelerator was released, which could be disconcerting when entering a corner. The steering wheel also tended to obscure the lower auxiliary gauges.

The second Sabre 6 roadster had the later round wheel arches and the optional hard-top that complemented the style very well. This example was the show car, seen here before the show stand was completed. Sadly, it lacks the wire wheels which add so much to the appeal of this sports car. The chrome grille and bumpers add to the quality aspect and once again the accuracy of the body shut-lines says a great deal for Reliant's expertise in the field of fibreglass moulding. Alas, this car seems to have disappeared.

Despite the fact that almost all the Sabre 4 cars were open two-seaters, Reliant only made two Sabre 6 drop-head cars which were distinguished from the four-cylinder versions by virtue of their horizontally slatted grilles. The first one still retained the square rear wheel arches and was also fitted with the swing-axle front suspension. The car seen here is without bumper trims or overriders and clearly is a prototype but handsome nevertheless, and it is sad that more were not made as it surely would have been eminent competition for the Austin-Healey and TR4. This car is still in running order in Leicestershire.

This view of the Reliant stand at the 1963 Motor Show features two Sabre 6 GTs, the white car in the foreground is chassis no. 120 and the white drop-head is chassis no. 122. By this time all these models were fitted with the later wishbone front suspension, seen on the rolling chassis mounted on a plinth behind the white fixed-head GT. According to club records, only this latter car seems to have survived.

Reliant believed in using their latest cars for their sales representatives and here we see the four main area salesmen alongside their Sabre 6 company cars. Left to right: Jim Lowrie from Scotland, Dermot Slater of Northern Counties, Hugh Baugh from the South and East and Bill Woolley from Eastern Counties. Of the cars, only DWD 234C and DWD 235C exist today.

Sales Manager Tom Scott (left) is demonstrating the revised Sabre 6 front suspension to Graham Robinson (far right), who was Competition Manager for Triumph at the time and later became a journalist and prolific author of motoring books.

This charming family photograph shows the late Joe Devlin with his wife, Mary, and their children polishing his beloved Sabre 6. Joe was an ex-Reliant employee and raced his Sabre at club events around the country and was a founding member of the Sabre and Scimitars Owners Club.

Many celebrities were attracted to the Sabre and here is (now Sir) Norman Wisdom with his newly acquired Sabre 6, although the name of his accomplice is not known, 1963. At this time there were very few sporting coupés of this type available and to some it assumed the role of the poor man's Aston Martin. Unfortunately, it was to very few as only seventy-seven Sabre 6 cars were made despite a very ambitious and not unsuccessful international rally career, which is explored in chapter two.

Reliant clearly did their utmost to publicise the Sabre 6 and here we see the Shadows group, including (now Sir) Cliff Richard, posing on a Sabre 6 outside the Pinewood Studios where the car featured in a film. The whereabouts of this car, as well as Norman Wisdom's car, is not known, which is all the more sad as they would, no doubt, be extremely valuable specimens today. As it is, the Sabre 6 languishes in esteem far behind other contemporary designs such as the Austin-Healey 3000, which in many ways were no superior on the road though perhaps were prettier in appearance.

CHAPTER TWO

RALLYING CALL

To enter works prepared cars into international rallying is a very brave move by any manufacturer as the reliability and performance of the product is fully exposed to the media and spectators. Success or failure can influence the level of sales to a marked extent, which is the gamble makers take intentionally having faith in their cars. It was especially brave for Reliant as they had never produced a sports car before or had any experience of preparing and running cars in rallies of any kind. In some ways they had everything to lose against the established competition, whose companies were far bigger and more experienced in motor sport as well as having far greater budgets. Despite this potential handicap, Reliant acquitted themselves reasonably well and probably gained support as a result of their courage in taking on such a daunting task.

Rallying is probably the oldest form of motorsport and from the beginning of the twentieth century has attracted the attention of car manufacturers as a means of developing and publicising the capabilities of their products. Such commercial involvement has usually been restricted to the larger manufacturers with sufficient reserves of cash to risk in this activity. The risks should not be underestimated as failure in this public form of competition can do far more harm to a company's reputation than not taking part at all.

Reliant was a very small manufacturer in the 1960s, compared with the big five car makers of the period who dominated the rallying world, namely Austin/Morris (BMC), Ford, Rootes, Standard and Triumph. The decision of Ray Wiggin to enter this competitive scene with Reliant's new sports car was typically brave, some at the time even said stupid. Arthur Rusling was chosen to manage the department and despite some misgivings about the competitiveness of the new models undertook the task in earnest by entering the first international event, the Tulip Rally of 1962, with himself in the navigator's seat. Even though he was unwell during that event, they did complete the course and from then on Arthur controlled the team from outside the competing vehicle, either travelling in another Sabre or the Ford Zephyr estate support car.

No less than four Sabre 4s were entered later in 1962 in the RAC Rally, which is a gruelling rally even for hardened competitors. Two of the Reliant contingent survived this testing event, during which much was learned about the problems resulting from the peculiar rear suspension, when the car was used on rough terrain after one car retired with rear axle failure. Undaunted, three of these works cars were entered in the 1963 Monte Carlo Rally in the full gaze of the international scene, as it was at the time the most prestigious rally of the year. Two of the three finished, with a third in class being recorded by Derrick Astle in 6 EUE.

Arthur Rusling realised that more power was required if the Sabres were to hope to appear on the results sheets and the introduction of the six-cylinder car later in 1963 was just what he had envisaged. Three of these new models were commandeered by the competitions department and modified to meet with the rivals from BMC in their Austin-Healeys. The front suspension was converted to the double wishbone system derived from Triumph TR4 components and a limited-slip differential was installed in the new Salisbury 7HA rear axle, which was also equipped with disc brakes from an Aston Martin DB4. Power from the Ford Zodiac engine was vastly increased by fitting a Raymond Mays alloy head conversion together with three twin-choke Weber 40DCOE carburettors. Finally, a strong Jaguar gearbox was grafted on to the engine to deal with the increased power and torque.

All three cars, registered 648, 649 and 650 GUE respectively, were entered in the 1963 Alpine Rally with one driven by a newcomer to the team, Roger Clark. Even though Clark and the other drivers complained about the performance of the new Sabre 6, Bobby Parkes in 649 GUE and Roger Clark in 650 GUE finished first and second in class respectively when all the Healeys failed to finish. This was indeed the model's one moment of glory and it set Roger Clark on his career as one of the most successful British rally drivers ever, even though he never drove for Reliant again after his criticisms of the car.

Rather rashly, perhaps, considering the unsuitability of the Sabre on rough roads, Rusling entered the three Sabre 6s on the notorious Spa–Sofia–Liège rally two months after the Alpine Rally. Not surprisingly all three retired, either because they crashed on leaving the road or the crew became exhausted. Raymond Baxter of BBC fame joined the team for this event and he was greatly relieved when his rally ended prematurely after the car left the road. He even offered to post his drenched underwear to Arthur Rusling!

Only two works cars were entered for the RAC Rally in November 1963, with stalwart Reliant driver Bobby Parkes in one and Raymond Baxter returning to the fray in the other. They were joined by two privately entered cars, a Sabre 4 driven by Leslie Griffiths from the West Country and a Sabre 6 driven by Graham P. Warner of Norfolk. Parkes and Griffiths finished third and sixth in their respective classes, while the two other Sabres succumbed to the ravages of this tough British event. The third works Sabre 6 was still being repaired after the Spa rally and while in the workshop at Tamworth two more headlamps were incorporated in the bonnet moulding to improve night visibility. This did not, however, improve the appearance of the cars. In 1964 the 648 GUE, with this equipment, was entered in the Welsh Rally to test the set-up, this outing resulted in a second in class for Bobby Parkes. The 649 and 650 GUE were similarly adapted with four headlamps for the 1964 Monte Carlo Rally. This ended with a fourth in class for Graham A. Warner in 650 GUE, but Bobby Parkes and Arthur Senior had a spectacular accident close to the finish which demolished the car but luckily not themselves. Graham P. Warner finished fifth in class in his privately entered Sabre 6. This was the last outing for the works Sabres and the remaining cars were sold off to private entrants and fortunately still survive to this day. Leslie Griffiths' son, Alex, continued in his father's footsteps by having a Sabre 6 prepared by the works for private use and entered the 1965 Monte Carlo rally, but unfortunately they retired on their maiden outing. This car has also survived the passage of time.

15 CUE was the first Sabre 4 fixed-head coupé, hence the rather unusual oval rear window which was not featured on any subsequent rallying version, thankfully! This car was also the first Sabre to enter rallying with works backing. The eventual competition manager, Arthur Rusling (with the bald head), is overseeing preparation of the car prior to its first outing in the 1962 Tulip Rally in Holland.

Summary of Rally Sabre Achievements

Event	Reg. No.	Driver/Co-Driver	No.	Result
Tulip Rally May 1962	15 CUE Sabre 4	Arthur Rusling Peter Easten	16	Retired
RAC Rally November 1962	42 ENX Sabre 4	Bob Aston Gerry Cooper	78	Thirty-fourth place
	15 CUE Sabre 4	Jimmy Ray John Hopwood	27	Thirty-eighth place
	7 EUE Sabre 4	Tony Fisher John King	36	Retired – rear axle
	6 EUE Sabre 4	Derrick Astle Peter Roberts	25	Retired
Monte Carlo Rally January 1963	6 EUE Sabre 4	Derrick Astle Peter Roberts	139	Third in class
	7 EUE Sabre 4	Tony Fisher David Skeffington	172	Ninety-second Hit church and damaged lights
	42 ENX Sabre 4	Jimmy Ray Mike Hughes	156	Retired
	342 ENX Regal three-wheeler	Cecil Sandford David Cooper		Press car
Circuit of Ireland April 1963	42 ENX Sabre 4	Tony Fisher Ronald Crellin		Third in class
Coupe des Alpes June 1963	648 GUE Sabre 6	Jimmy Ray Peter Roberts	1	Retired – hit tree at half-way
	650 GUE Sabre 6	Roger Clark Bob Aston	2	Second in class
	649 GUE Sabre 6	Bobby Parkes Gerry Cooper	3	First in class
Spa–Sofia–Liège August 1963	649 GUE Sabre 6	Bobby Parkes Arthur Senior	6	Retired – hit wolf at 100mph
	648 GUE Sabre 6	Raymond Baxter Douglas Wilson-Spratt	7	Retired – hit bollard, left road
	650 GUE Sabre 6	Robin Richards Alec Lobb	114	Retired – crew fatigue
RAC Rally November 1963	649 GUE Sabre 6	Bobby Parkes Roy Dixon	16	Third in unlimited GT class
	650 GUE	Raymond Baxter	18	Retired – burst tyre,

	Sabre 6	Ernest McMillen		in ditch
	42 ENX	Leslie Griffiths	69	Private entry, sixth in
	Sabre 4	Stuart Turner		class, sixty-fifth overall
	WGV 287	Graham P. Warner	176	Private entry, retired
	Sabre 6	John Spiers		
Monte Carlo Rally	649 GUE	Bobby Parkes	263	Retired – fell 70ft
January 1964	Sabre 6	Arthur Senior		30 miles from finish
	650 GUE	Graham A. Warner	247	Fourth in class,
	Sabre 6	Peter Roberts		ninety-fourth overall
	WGV 287	Graham P. Warner	43	Private entry, 5th in
	Sabre 6	John Spiers		class, 158th overall
Welsh Rally	648 GUE	Bobby Parkes	12	Second in class,
January 1964		Peter Roberts		fourteenth overall
	42 ENX	Alex Griffiths	29	Private entry, first in
	Sabre 4	Stuart Turner		class, thirteenth overall
Monte Carlo Rally	660 XYB	Alex Griffiths	99	Private entry, retired
January 1965	Sabre 6	Stuart Turner		

Arthur Rusling navigated 15 CUE on its first international rally accompanying the experienced privateer Peter Easten. They did not finish that event, as Arthur was unwell, but were sufficiently encouraged by the car's performance on that smooth event to enter the RAC Rally later that year. This time John Hopwood navigated Jimmy Ray and during a rough stage on the rally the windscreen landed intact on John's lap, much to his consternation! Hence the black tape round the screen in this shot after they had replaced it.

The typical rough sections of the RAC Rally are well illustrated here as 15 CUE continues unabated after the replacement of the errant windscreen, eventually achieving thirty-eighth place overall.

Reliant entered no less than four Sabre 4s in the 1962 RAC Rally and here two of them (6 EUE and 7 EUE) are being prepared at the factory development shop. Note the studded tyres stacked in the background which were used on icy sections and sometimes in conjunction with chains, which were used on car 25.

Another scene from the 1962 RAC Rally on a typical forestry section in which 6 EUE is going well, here driven by Derrick Astle, although the car later retired with rear axle problems. Derrick went on to drive for BMC in an Austin-Healey 3000 but sadly was killed while driving one in the 1963 Tulip Rally.

Immediately after the RAC Rally 6 EUE and sister car 7 EUE are being prepared for the first Monte Carlo Rally Reliant had entered, in 1963. They also entered another Sabre 4, 42 ENX, as well as a three-wheeled Regal for a press crew.

6 EUE is climbing the famous Col de Turini just above Monte Carlo. Derrick Astle is driving in his last event for Reliant and did reasonably well to come third in class, particularly as this was Reliant's first attempt at the Monte Carlo Rally. This car and 7 EUE were sold, for £700 each, to private enthusiasts after this event as Reliant developed later models for competition.

The Col de Turini is again the backdrop for this photograph of 7 EUE competing in the 1963 Monte Carlo Rally and driven by Tony Fisher and photographer David Skeffington. They finished ninety-second after hitting a church which damaged their lights.

42 ENX, seen here in the Maritime Alps in southern France on the 1963 Monte Carlo Rally, has clearly had mild contact with a snow bank at the front. The crew of Jimmy Ray and Mike Hughes, the navigator, eventually retired. Reliant sold the car to one of its dealers in Bristol after the event and it appeared regularly alongside the works cars in later rallies.

In 1963 Reliant had the Sabre 6 in their range, and this car was soon adopted by the competition department for rallying. Their first event was the prestigious Alpine Rally, or Coupe des Alpes, where they were in the same class as the all-conquering Austin-Healey 3000 cars from BMC. 649 GUE was driven by Bobby Parkes, who went on to drive for Reliant in every subsequent event after winning his class in this event.

650 GUE storming through a French village on the Alpine Rally of 1963 with Roger Clark at the wheel, already demonstrating his characteristic opposite-lock style of driving which was frowned upon at that time. Together with 649 GUE, they took the top two places in the over 2½ litre class against the fancied big Healeys, all of which retired. This was certainly Reliant's most successful showing in the world of international rallying.

650 GUE was one of three Sabre 6s developed by the competition department in time for the 1963 Alpine event and is seen here driven by someone who later became a famous Ford rally competitor, Roger Clark. This was his first 'works' drive ever, and his last for Reliant when he complained about the poor performance of the car, despite the fact that he came second in class behind another Sabre, 649 GUE.

The third of the Sabre 6 team cars being driven by the BBC commentator Raymond Baxter, who had driven for other works teams including Rootes before this 1963 Spa–Sofia–Liège Rally. Whereas the Alpine Rally was largely a smooth road event, the very rough terrain of the Spa–Sofia–Liège event did not suit the unyielding nature of the Sabre suspension and all three cars retired as a result of leaving the road. Raymond Baxter expressed great relief when his drive was over.

Raymond Baxter took the helm of 650 GUE for the 1963 RAC Rally because his previous mount, 648 GUE, was still being repaired and Roger Clark had moved on to drive for Rover in their new 2000 model, 1 KUE. Sadly his rally yet again ended in a ditch after a tyre burst and he did not appear in a Sabre again.

Bobby Parkes driving 649 GUE at the 1963 RAC Rally following his class win in the Alpine Rally and retirement from the Spa–Sofia–Liège Rally. He was again the most successful of the total of four Sabres entering this event, coming third in the unlimited GT class. The rough nature of the RAC was again a problem for the Sabres causing two of the other cars to retire.

Reliant dealer Leslie Griffiths, from near Bristol, with 42 ENX awaiting the start of another stage of the 1963 RAC Rally. 42 ENX had been previously entered by the works in the 1962 RAC Rally, 1963 Circuit of Ireland and 1963 Monte Carlo Rally before being sold to Leslie Griffiths. His navigator in the 1963 event was no less than Stuart Turner, who later became Competition Manager at Ford.

The rough nature of the RAC Rally is very evident here with Leslie Griffiths driving his ex-works Sabre 4 in his first international event with the car. This car had entered more rallies than any of the other Sabres and the level of modification it received enabled it to tackle rough stages with greater reliability.

No amount of development can prevent the sort of damage incurred by 42 ENX later in the 1963 RAC Rally when it hit some logs during a forest stage. Despite damaging two wire wheels and bending the rear axle, which had to be changed, the crew of Griffiths and Turner managed to finish sixty-fifth overall. Leslie eventually handed over 42 ENX to his son Alex to drive in future events.

While 648 GUE was being repaired after the Spa–Sofia–Liège Rally, Arthur Rusling decided to follow BMC's lead and build in a pair of extra halogen headlamps to improve visibility on night stages. The car first appeared in this guise at the 1964 Welsh Rally when Bobby Parkes piloted the car to second in class and fourteenth overall. He was just beaten, by one position, by Alex Griffiths in his ex-works Sabre 4, which said a great deal about the latter car's performance and the new young owner's abilities.

The other two works Sabre 6s were also fitted with modified bonnets following the experiment with 648 GUE and these two cars were entered in the 1964 Monte Carlo Rally. This was much against the wishes of Arthur Rusling who felt the cars were not ideal for this event, but Ray Wiggin insisted that the rally offered unrivalled publicity. Graham A. Warner is seen here in 650 GUE and eventually finished fourth in class.

Bobby Parkes was back in his original Sabre, 649 GUE for the 1964 Monte Carlo Rally, seen here for the last time in one piece. Together with Arthur Senior as navigator they were doing well in their class until 30 miles from the finish . . .

The wreck of the 649 GUE. During the road sections linking the timed stages on international rallies it is quite common for the navigator to take the helm to allow the main driver some rest. So it was that Arthur Senior was driving 649 GUE into Monte Carlo for the final test when some 30 miles from their destination he overshot a hairpin – navigators also get tired during these events! The consequent 70ft drop down the mountainside back on to the road they would have eventually driven along spelled the death knell for car no. 263, but fortunately not for the occupants. Such was the strength of the Sabre chassis both walked away from the wreckage with nothing more than superficial wounds.

This amusing cartoon illustrates the final journey of 649 GUE, which is the only works car not to survive to this day.

One feature of the Monte Carlo Rally was the various starting points available, making it very much a gamble as to which would be the most advantageous, depending on weather conditions. In 1964, private entrants Graham P. Warner (not to be confused with Graham A. Warner) and John Spiers chose Minsk in Russia. This is probably the first time a Sabre had ever been seen in that country. They finished the rally fifth in class having followed a very icy route, as one might have expected.

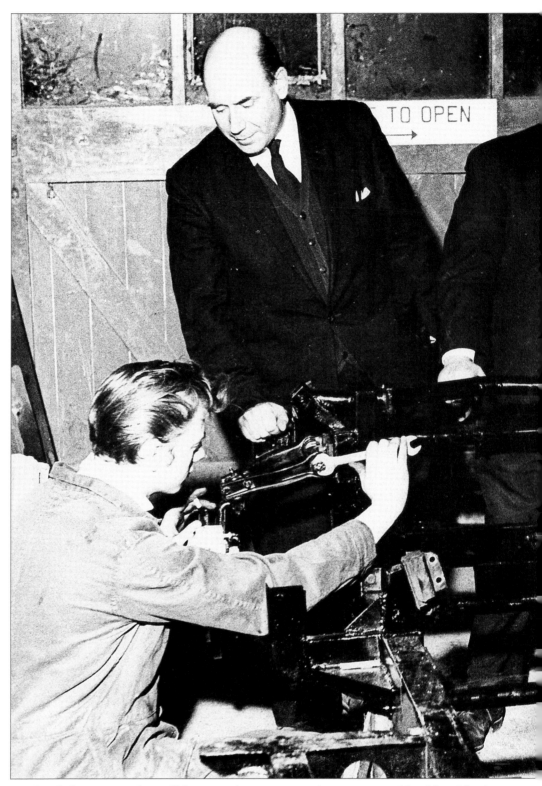

Another dealer entrant, Alex Griffiths, is seen here inspecting the preparation of his Sabre 6 for the 1965 Monte Carlo Rally. The works abandoned their rallying exploits in 1964 after that fateful event but nevertheless supported other entries technically, as in this case. The car registered

660 XYB did not finish this winter event but is now used in historic rallies by its Warwickshire owner, Richard Prosser.

One or two private Sabres were entered in international rallies, usually by enthusiastic dealers with previous rallying experience. One such driver was Graham P. Warner who campaigned WGV 287 in the 1963 RAC Rally where he retired. Here he is seen at the 1964 Monte Carlo Rally where he came fifth in class. This car now resides in Northern Ireland.

One very special Sabre 6, 876 HWD, was constructed with racing in mind and initially it was used by Bobby Parkes in hill climbs, and later by Robin Rew, seen racing here. Modifications were made by David Page to incorporate a double wishbone independent rear suspension system and a five-speed ZF gearbox similar to that used in Alvis 3 litre cars. The rear wing shape was widened and flattened to accommodate the new rear track and it was rumoured that an entry for the Le Mans 24 Hour Race was envisaged.

The engines of the rally Sabres and 876 HWD were fitted with Raymond Mays aluminium twelve-port cylinder heads and equipped with three 45 DCOE Weber carburettors. Reliant never really succeeded in obtaining the maximum benefit from this set up and it was not until subsequent owners acquired examples, such as Robin Rew who campaigned HWD for many years, that the true potential of this car was realised.

In addition to rallying, Graham P. Warner, whose garage was in Bury St Edmunds, decided to contest the Commander's Cup at the nearby circuit at Snetterton. This was an endurance race run over twenty-four hours and Graham chose a standard showroom car, WGT 889, and during May 1964 the team of drivers, under the supervision of Arthur Rusling, completed the twenty-four hours at an average speed of 70.18mph. The only problems were overheating, cured by removing the thermostat, and wire wheel spokes breaking due to the continuous high-speed cornering.

This pit stop during the Commanders Cup was also a driver change with Mike Watts taking over. The only modification made to the Sabre was fitting iodine vapour lights for the night section. This was effectively a mini Le Mans and was a creditable achievement with a perfectly standard car as opposed to a specially built racer, the type normally entered in the French endurance race.

Another survivor, 648 GUE, was found and restored by Robin Rew and is seen here competing at Barbon Hill Climb in Lancashire, 1978. The car has had various owners since, and even spent some time in Japan, from whence it has fortunately returned for another rebuild.

This much used ex-works Sabre 4 is seen in full flight in a Coronation Rally on the Eppynt Ranges in South Wales in the early 1980s. It was driven by John Valler who crashed it later in the event and the car is now undergoing a protracted restoration in Sussex. The other two rally Sabre 4s, 6 and 7 EUE are slowly being restored by their owners in Essex and Cornwall respectively.

A number of Sabres have been used in recent years in historic rallying and racing and one of the most successful was again a car owned initially by Robin Rew and subsequently developed into a very competitive hill-climb car by myself, seen here at Shelsley Walsh, 1983. 92 FRP held a class record at Prescott for seventeen years from 1982 until 1999.

Incredibly all the works rally cars apart from 649 GUE have survived to this day. Here we see Roger Clark's old car, 650 GUE, being used in an autotest by its present owner Roger Heron. The car still retains the Jaguar overdrive gearbox Reliant fitted to some of the rally cars out of fear of overstressing the Ford unit.

CHAPTER THREE

SCIMITAR IS BORN

The very first Ogle-designed Scimitar Coupé, which was actually registered as an Ogle. The car was used as the subject for the sales brochure and as a test bed by Reliant. They also lent it to various journalists to test privately, and one, Edward Eves of Autocar magazine, was very influential in suggesting modifications to the rear suspension which Reliant readily carried out after about sixty models had been produced. The size and enthusiasm of the company management allowed such modifications to be made with minimum loss of time and expense.

Any motor-car manufacturer that had struggled to sell just over 130 examples of a new sporting model over a period of 3 years might well have been justified in pulling the plug and changing course in the light of market forces. It seems that Reliant, under the management of Ray Wiggin and his Sales Director Tom Scott, were made of sterner stuff. Despite great efforts in international rallying on a very limited budget and with some success, sales of the Sabres just did not take off as they should. Objectively, one has to conclude that two factors possibly mitigated against a more successful outcome from the efforts of the Reliant team. Firstly, the appearance of the Sabres was not to everyone's taste and neither was the handling, and, second, the idea of fibreglass bodywork still had the image of kit-car and amateur-build quality. There was no possibility of Reliant employing anything other than GRP as a body material and Jensen had already entered the field at a higher price level with their 541 model, made from similar material with slightly more success. However, body design and handling properties were factors that could and should have been addressed and were within the capability of the company. Inspiration was the missing ingredient and fortunately this came at the 1963 Motor Show in the form of the Daimler SX250 exhibited on the Ogle Design stand. An elegant 2+2 coupé had been commissioned by the Helena Rubenstein cosmetic company to be fitted to the Daimler SP250 chassis and the finished product was on display at Earl's Court. Only two cars were ever made, the second being ordered by Boris Forter, who established the British branch of Helena Rubenstein.

Ray Wiggin spotted the exhibit and was deeply impressed by it. Further enquiries revealed that the future of the Daimler-based car was most uncertain as far as future production was concerned and negotiations about its possible application to a Reliant model were soon under way. Initial measurements indicated that the body would be an almost perfect fit for the Sabre 6 chassis dimensions and very quickly a deal was struck to pursue the idea of fitting the new Ogle coupé body to the Reliant base unit. While the merger of the two assemblies was not entirely straightforward, the efforts were certainly promising and a prototype was constructed and registered as an Ogle with the number AUE 38B. Few external changes were made from the original Ogle design apart from the rear wheel-arch shape which became round instead of flattened at the top while the fuel filler was placed on the nearside rear pillar instead of below the rear window. Front and rear bumpers were now of a rounder section derived from the Ford Classic Capri GT, as was the windscreen. Reliant were entering a different section of the car market as the new model was not a pure sports car but a Grand Touring car capable of carrying four persons, at a pinch, and sufficient luggage and fuel (20 gallons no less) on long journeys. However, its 100+mph performance still qualified it as a sporting machine since the venerable Ford straight six 2553cc engine was now equipped with three SU carburettors on a Reliant-designed manifold producing 120bhp. On paper the new Scimitar Coupé was now a force to be reckoned with, as the figures below indicate and it even compares favourably with the Datsun 280ZX produced fourteen years later:

	Price (£)	Max. Speed (mph)	0–60mph (secs)	50–70mph in top gear (secs)	mpg
Scimitar	1,292	117	11.4	7.7	19.8
Healey 3000	1,106	121	9.8	7.9	20.3

Daimler SP250	1,395	121	10.2	7.8	29.1
Datsun 280ZX (1979)	6,927	117	10.4	11.6	19.5
	(1979 price)				

The handling of the new car still attracted comment from the press as the suspension design was carried over from the Sabre 6, mainly unaltered. Suggestions from *Autocar*'s Midland editor, Edward Eves, were taken on board and David Page, Engineering Director at Reliant, designed a revised layout involving twin trailing arms and a watt linkage fixed to the differential casing to afford perfect lateral location for the rear axle. This move transformed the predictability of the car's road-holding and was incorporated after sixty cars had been made. A total of 296 Scimitar Coupés were fitted with the straight-six engine, the model being termed the SE4, before a change was made to the V6 3 litre Ford engine in line with Ford model changes. The revised SE4a incorporated a few minor suspension changes resulting in a lower roll centre at the front and the introduction of a front anti-roll bar to balance this move. Power output was now increased to 130bhp resulting in an even more competitive straight-line performance against its rivals, as the *Autocar* figures below illustrate:

	Price (£)	Max. Speed (mph)	0–60mph (secs)	50–70mph in top gear (secs)	mpg
V6 Scimitar	1,516	121	10.0	6.3	22.1
Austin-Healey 3000 Mk III	1,126	121	9.8	7.9	20.3
Sunbeam Tiger	1,471	117	9.5	6.8	16.9
Alfa Romeo 2600	3,051	117	11.7	7.9	17.7

The handling was now very acceptable and well up to the standards of the opposition but the decision to return to steel wheels instead of the handsome wire variety fitted to the earlier SE4 cars was a very sad one and did not enhance the appeal of the car at all in the showroom. The interior also suffered from the contemporary trend for all black trim. This was far less attractive than the fascia and seat design of the straight-six car, which used mock wood on the fascia and cloth inserts on the seats, features added by other manufacturers twenty years later.

In September 1967 Reliant introduced a 2.5 litre version of the Scimitar Coupé as a more economic model in view of the petrol crisis at the time. When *Autocar* tested this version, known as the SE4b, they recorded a maximum speed of 111mph and a fuel consumption figure of 23mpg, which was hardly a startling improvement and only 117 of these cars were sold out of the 700 V6 cars made.

A very interesting and significant version of the straight-six Coupé was the Ogle Triplex GTS, commissioned by Triplex to demonstrate their new tinted, laminated and heated automotive glass. This estate version of the Coupé, built by Ogle, was shown at the 1965 Motor Show and caught the eye of the Duke of Edinburgh, among many others. After it was also exhibited at the Turin Motor Show he eventually borrowed it for his personal transport for two years. This development did a great deal for the reputation of Reliant, since they were the makers of the base vehicle, but little for Triplex who had ordered and paid for its production in the hope of demonstrating their new glass technology around the world. In 1967 the GTS was handed over to the National Motor Museum at Beaulieu for permanent exhibition there until 1988 when the museum decided to return it to the original owners, Triplex Glass. They in turn sold it to me after protracted negotiations. The history of this car started royal patronage of Scimitars that persists to this day with the Princess Royal owning the last version of the marque.

Less significant variants of the Coupé were made, including one by John Crosthwaite who was recruited to take charge of chassis design. This car was developed after the introduction of the GTE and was based on a shortened version of the GTE chassis with the front bodywork from the later model and front-mounted spare wheel. Only recently a drop-head version was built by Scimpart which demonstrated what a handsome car evolved from the basic shape when the roof was removed. How sad Reliant did not think of the idea in the 1960s as it would have surely expanded the appeal of the car to a much wider audience. However, as we shall see in the next chapter, the eventual development of the Coupé into the GTE was by far the best move ever made by the Reliant management.

The Ogle SX250 was a specially commissioned fibreglass-bodied Coupé, designed and built by David Ogle Ltd based on the Daimler SP250 sports car whose bodywork was also GRP. Tom Karen of Ogle styled the car for Rubenstein cosmetic company and it was exhibited at the 1962 Motor Show. Ray Wiggin of Reliant was very taken with the looks of this elegant car.

Since sales of the Sabre 6 were very disappointing, Ray Wiggin was on the lookout for a more attractive body design in the hope of stimulating the interest that the rally exploits had failed to do. Some quick measurements revealed that the SX250 body would fit the Sabre 6 chassis dimensions almost perfectly. Since the SX250 project ended with only two examples Reliant were able to complete a deal to adopt the design with suitable modifications and the Scimitar seen here was born.

Apart from structural alterations required to fit the chassis shape of the Sabre 6, externally the front headlamp arrangement was more curvaceous, as was the Ford Classic derived bumper and windscreen, and blended well with the profile of the rest of the car. The headlamp bezels were modelled on the recently introduced Triumph 2000 and the side/indicator lights came from the Austin-Healey Sprite. The wire wheels suited the clean body shape perfectly.

Changes to the rear bodywork of the SX250 car involved more rounded wheel arches, again to match the shape of the profile. The rear bumper came from the same source as the front one but retained the wrap-around section, removed at the front. It also had a slightly flatter profile, achieved by cutting and rejoining the bumper at the centre, also necessary to match the width of the car.

The new Scimitar provided a very good seating position for a driver of any height, with well-positioned steering wheel and instruments. The front seats reclined as well as tipping forward for easier access to the rather confined rear bench seat. The recessed door panel housed a lidded glove compartment and the leather-covered interior handle was ideally placed.

This interior shot of the Scimitar Coupé shows the comprehensive instrumentation, rather better laid out than in the Sabre. The formica wood-effect fascia was characteristic of that period but the leather-bound steering wheel, gear knob and door knobs are high-grade features, as are the supportive seats trimmed in vinyl with cloth inserts. The overall effect was impressive from such a small manufacturer with no experience in the luxury GT field.

Only fifty-nine cars had been produced by the time the rear suspension was modified and this car, seen at the Motor Show, must be a later example of the straight-six Scimitar Coupé chassis as the twin trailing arms are clearly visible. The top trailing arm on each side was slightly kinked in order to clear the rear seat pan when the suspension was fully compressed. The earlier arrangement also tended to twist the axle under roll conditions and this was now eliminated to give the axle tubes a longer life expectancy.

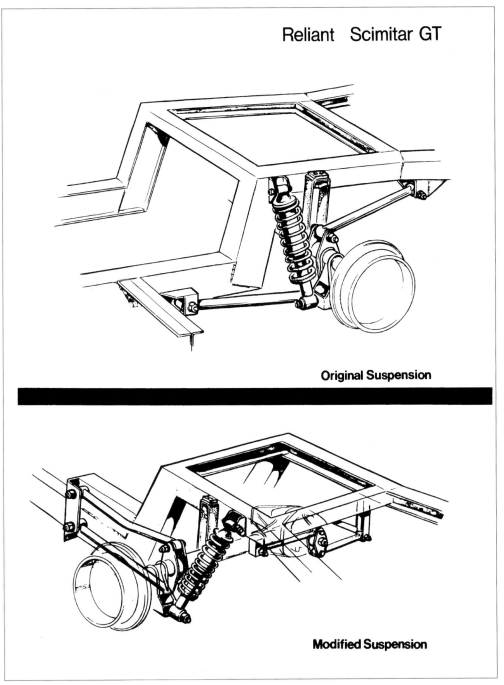

Reliant   Scimitar GT

Original Suspension

Modified Suspension

Initial press comments about the new Scimitar were largely favourable, particularly regarding the styling and refined accommodation. However, the suspension was virtually unchanged from the Sabre 6, on which the car was based. The main weakness of this design was in the rear suspension, itself a legacy of the need to utilise components purchased in the initial deal with Les Ballamy. The Midland editor of *Autocar*, Edward Eves, was an early user of the new Scimitar and he conveyed his feelings about the deficiencies of the rear axle location to Reliant and suggested a revision on the lines of the Aston Martin DB2-4. Reliant went one stage further and introduced a transverse Watt linkage to the backplate of the rear differential, thus achieving the ideal geometry. This design, refined by John Crosthwaite, was retained until the end of Scimitar production some twenty years later and the transformation is illustrated in these diagrams.

This shows Reliant's primitive method of testing for water leaks in each production vehicle. By today's standards this apparatus leaves something to be desired in its ability to confirm the water tightness of door and window seals and the subsequent owners had really to prove this aspect for themselves on the open road. However, each car was given a test run before dispatch and they were hand-built cars in the true sense of the words, so tolerances did vary accordingly.

Reliant are probably the most experienced producers of GRP car bodies in the world and here we see a mould of the rear section of a Coupé being dismantled after the moulding process has cured. This reveals the crude bodyshell which has then to be finished by hand where the mould joins and then at the edges. Reliant never used self-coloured resins in finished colour and the cars were always sprayed finally in conventional cellulose.

The production rate of the Scimitar Coupé was far greater than the Sabre and began at the rate of about eight to ten cars a week. The cars were all hand-built, as can be seen from this picture, and the occasional vehicle had an electrically operated sun roof fitted – a very advanced feature in the early 1960s. The straight six Ford engine was retained for the Scimitar Coupé for the first 296 models until Ford replaced it with a V6 unit.

Prince Philip arriving at London Airport with the Triplex Ogle GTS, which heralded an ongoing line of Royal Scimitars. Triplex had intended to send their project Ogle car around the world's motor shows but only managed to send it to Turin after Earl's Court because the Duke of Edinburgh requested to use it as his personal car. He was obviously fascinated by it and considered it an ideal replacement for his Lagonda 3 litre.

In 1965 Triplex Glass Company commissioned Ogle to produce a project car to demonstrate their newly developed tinted, laminated Sundym automobile glass. Having just completed the Scimitar GT, Ogle chose it as a basis for such a project since it was so easy to modify fibreglass bodywork by

cutting out sections or bonding in new shapes. With the assistance of selected Reliant personnel the Triplex Ogle GTS was conceived in the form of an estate-car conversion.

In addition to the normal glass side windows Ogle also incorporated a bonded-in glass section to the roof above the two front seats. Furthermore, both front and rear screens were heated by electric elements fixed between the two laminates of glass. The idea of using such elements in rear screens soon followed in other production cars, but it took thirty years before such a facility became an option in the front screen of production cars. This unique car was shown at the 1965 London Motor Show before being driven to Turin in Italy for the Motor Show there in a bid to attract more international customers.

Prince Philip returned the car to Triplex after two years and since its commercial potential was now redundant they loaned it to the National Motor Museum at Beaulieu. Here it is handed over to Lord Montagu (far right) in the presence of Ray Wiggin (second, left) and its designer Tom Karen (third, left), before I purchased it eight years later. Triplex Marketing Director Anthony Cleminson is second on the right.

When Ford replaced the straight-six engine with the 3 litre V6 unit, Reliant had to adjust the Scimitar Coupé bodyshell to accept it, together with a new gearbox and different rear axle. Since the new engine was shorter than the in-line one it was possible to mount it further back in the chassis which helped the weight distribution somewhat, even though accessibility to the various parts of the engine were not improved. The increase in power and torque markedly improved performance.

Externally Reliant did very little to distinguish the new V6 SE4/4A models and by fitting steel wheels instead of the more expensive wire variety they diminished the attractiveness of the car. However, with the aid of John Crosthwaite, who had worked for BRM among others, they improved both front and rear suspension geometries and added a front anti-roll to balance the lowered roll centre to the benefit of the handling.

The interior design was also altered, which in many eyes was not beneficial as they abandoned the variety of texture used in the original version in favour of entirely black vinyl trim coverings. Fortunately, they did not alter the excellent instrument layout and back seat room was marginally improved.

Despite the fitment of steel wheels with chrome embellishers, the Scimitar Coupé was still a very elegant shape and, combined with the effortless 120mph performance from the relatively large but unstressed engine, proved to be a fine grand touring car in the true sense. Eventually, over a thousand V6 Coupés were sold, which was a vast improvement compared with Reliant's previous sporting cars.

The chassis of the Scimitar was of very robust construction with good cross bracing and rigid front and rear suspension support sections. Together with excellent suspension geometry from the Triumph-based front wishbone and coil-spring set up, and Reliant's own twin trailing arm and lateral watt linkage for the rear axle, a car with exceptional road-holding for its day was produced.

The V6 engine was a very popular unit for the engine tuners because it was a lazy but torquey engine in standard form. Here is seen one of the more extreme modifications involving the fitting of triple Weber DCN carburettors on a special manifold which together with suitable camshaft and cylinder head changes could produce about 200bhp compared with the standard 140bhp output.

Reliant never produced an open version of the Coupé which was rather a shame as a recent private conversion by Scimpart Ltd illustrates what a pleasant car it would have been. The chassis was already very rigid in the beam section but this conversion involved adding reinforced sill and rear-bumper support sections to ensure lack of distortion or undue shake. The red leather trim and walnut fascia added considerable appeal to this basically elegant car and the rear overriders from a Sunbeam Alpine gave the rear end a less bland appearance as well as some protection.

This Scimitar Roadster, as it was called, was used on classic tours and at the occasional classic car show, but proved very usable and always attracted much attention, which indicates how successful it would have been if Reliant had pursued this course in the 1960s.

While John Crosthwaite was working at Reliant he carried out some interesting work with a view to extending the Coupé's versatility. Although the basic bodyshell was retained, a new front was grafted on from the later GTE model, which was slightly neater in appearance. This modification also allowed the spare wheel to be fitted in front of the engine and above the lowered radiator, as in the Ford Zodiac Mk IV from which the first Ford V6 came. The chassis was redesigned to allow the footwells to fit in between the chassis rails instead of above, thus providing more leg room.

This rear view shows the combined rear light units borrowed from the Hillman Hunter range and a central rear fuel filler now that the fuel tank was at the rear in place of the spare wheel. Removal of the fuel tank from behind the rear seat gave increased volume to the boot even though it was perhaps a less safe layout if the car was severely damaged at the rear. John Crosthwaite used this as a personal car for himself and his wife, and he fitted automatic transmission as she preferred it.

CHAPTER FOUR

THE GTE – THE FIRST SPORTING ESTATE CAR

The Scimitar GTE was a most revolutionary shape, particularly in profile, and this dramatic sales photograph, sub-titled 'Vroomy' and featuring the Red Arrows, was most eye-catching and appropriate. The combination of pace and space had not been achieved before in quite such a stylish package and the formula proved to be a winning one for Reliant who struggled to meet demand within a few years of its announcement.

After three years of production the Scimitar Coupé had established itself in a limited way as a worthy, fast and entertaining motor car of some elegance but perhaps lacking a little in versatility and accommodation. However, it was very much a sporting car with enough performance to embarrass many two-seater sports cars. In order to expand their market Ray Wiggin realised that Reliant needed a model with more room and a distinctive style. Motor shows are always good hunting grounds for inspiration and at this juncture the Lamborghini Espada caught Wiggin's attention as being a suitable format for his next model, and he duly requested Tom Karen of Ogle to come up with some ideas along those lines. Within weeks Karen had produced some drawings based on his previous designs for an Anadol estate, which Reliant were working on for their Turkish customers. The Triplex GTS had already sown the seeds of an estate concept for the Scimitar and so the revolutionary GTE (Grand Touring Estate) design evolved incorporating some ground-breaking features in automobile body design. Notable among these were the rising window line towards the rear, the lip above the rear window as an early form of spoiler and the split folding rear seats, which have since been copied almost universally in modern hatchbacks. The opening rear window was not unique but most practical and elegantly conceived. Thus the whole design still looked sporting but also encompassed the practicality of an estate car. With characteristic decisiveness, Ray Wiggin gave an immediate go-ahead for the GTE concept.

The new car really needed a new chassis and here the new Engineering Director John Crosthwaite started with a clean sheet of paper to produce the cruciform backbone and perimeter rail chassis, not unlike the Triumph Herald series, but retaining the solid rear axle, with longer trailing arms than the Coupé and wider track all round for greater stability. The new design allowed passenger footwells to be placed within the chassis members thus accommodating four adult passengers while only increasing the length of the car by 3in. Luggage room was vastly increased by placing the spare wheel in front of the radiator (like the Ford Zodiac Mk IV from which the engine came) so releasing space under the rear compartment for a 17 gallon fuel tank, some 3 gallons less than the Coupé. Clever design allowed the windscreen, doors and rear bumper of the Coupé to be carried over on to the new GTE, or SE5 as it was termed. In every other respect, apart from engine and gearbox, this was an entirely new car and was one of the stars of the 1968 Motor Show where a sectioned model was exhibited.

Ogle went one stage further by showing an even more dramatic version of the new concept at the same exhibition. This unique car incorporated a glass roof section above the front seats on the lines of the Triplex GTS and covers on the headlamps, which retracted when the lights were switched on. The interior was trimmed in patterned cloth for extra comfort. This car was acquired by Mr Julian Hodge, whose company, The Hodge Group, owned Reliant at the time, for his wife's use. The Hodge family still retain the vehicle, and it has been sympathetically restored.

Press opinion on the shape of the new Scimitar was divided quite markedly between admiration and guarded comments. However, once they had driven the vehicle most journalists were unstinting in their praise of its performance, handling and unique versatility compared with its rivals. The following results of *Motor* road tests make very interesting comparisons:

	Max. Speed (mph)	0–60mph (secs)	50–70mph in top gear (secs)	mpg
Scimitar GTE	113	10.2	7.5	19.2
Alfa 1750 GTV	115.5	9.3	8.0	23.4
Triumph TR6	117	8.5	8.0	20.8
Ford Capri 3000	114	9.5	6.4	19.7

While the 3 litre Capri was clearly its closest rival, the Scimitar scored highly on versatility, road-handling and exclusivity.

As with many entirely new designs the early customers experienced some snags that the development department had not discovered and the GTE was no exception. Comments about the early cars were concerned with the bodywork as the suspension design and running gear had already served the Coupé for a couple of years. The fuel filler was one of the first causes for complaint since it featured a right-angled hose between the vertical cap and the horizontal tank, which made refuelling slow and tiresome especially as it had a 17 gallon capacity. This was soon changed to an angled side-opening cap with a direct 2in feed pipe into the tank. Again at the rear of the car the opening window soon became very dirty in bad weather reducing rear vision to virtually nothing apart from optional door mirrors. Reliant introduced one of the first rear-window wash-wipe systems in a production car to solve this problem, since copied by every hatchback and estate car in modern production. The first seventeen cars also featured an elaborate spring-loaded system of rods to support this opening window, but this was replaced by the now ubiquitous gas strut, again pioneered by Reliant on this model. Initially, all cars were fitted with the Ford four-speed gearbox in conjunction with a Laycock LH overdrive on third and fourth gears. In 1970 a Borg-Warner 35 automatic bax was available as an option intended for the executive buyer, who was now becoming attracted to this exciting car.

By the end of 1969 740 SE5 models had been made and a further 1,000 were manufactured in 1970. The capacity of the Tamworth factory was now being stretched and as sales of the Coupé were rapidly declining this model was dropped in favour of the GTE, which received its first face-lift in October 1971. Revisions included a one-piece cast front grille and removal of the waistline chrome strip in favour of a painted coachline. Badges and lettering were given a new wider form and aluminium trims were added to the lower part of the sill. More subtle was the raising of the headlamps by a few inches to comply with new lighting regulations. Inside a radical make-over included replacing all the hand-trimmed panels with moulded ABS versions which gave the car a more modern appearance. However, these changes have made the SE5a models far more difficult to restore when these parts eventually become brittle and crack or distort after many years of use and abuse.

A further 2,500 cars were made in the next twelve months, by which time the V6 engine was revised when the Ford Granada was introduced. A slight power increase was now on offer and small changes to the front suspension geometry accompanied this move. Unfortunately, Ford decided to abandon the overdrive gearbox at this juncture leaving Reliant little option but to follow suit and adopt the new Granada box allied to a higher 3.07 rear axle ratio to compensate for the lack of overdrive.

The consequence was a much higher bottom gear, a far nicer gearchange and surprisingly even better performance, as shown below:

	Max. Speed (mph)	0–60mph (secs)	50–70mph in top gear (secs)	mpg
SE5a manual	121	8.5	10.1	20.8

Production now averaged fifty cars a week and this sometimes rose to seventy. In order to achieve this rate the GRP bodyshells had to be cured in low temperature ovens to keep up with assembly demands. Unfortunately, this had an adverse effect, with some rippling occurring in the gel coat, particularly noticeable above and behind the front wheel arch, for some reason, on 1974–5-built cars. Reliant addressed the lack of overdrive by commissioning an outside firm, Rugby Autocars, to assemble gearboxes based on the Ford V4 Transit, which would fit the V6 block, but with Granada internals and a special output shaft to match the later Laycock J-type overdrive. Such an assembly but with different ratios was used in the Ford 3 litre Transits used by the police and ambulance services. Reliant had to employ the remote gear linkage from the early 3 litre Capris which also used this box initially but without overdrive. The quality of the gearchange was markedly inferior to the manual non-overdrive cars but the versatility of six speeds and clutchless gearchanges on the upper two ratios was considered worthwhile compensation. Ironically, the maximum speed of the latest overdrive version of the SE5a was not as fast as the non-overdrive version and there was only a marginal improvement in the mpg figure over the four-speed car, although cruising was a more relaxed affair in the later car.

Demand began to fall off during 1975 but luckily Reliant had a replacement model planned for the Motor Show that year, with which they hoped to restore interest in this niche area of the automobile market.

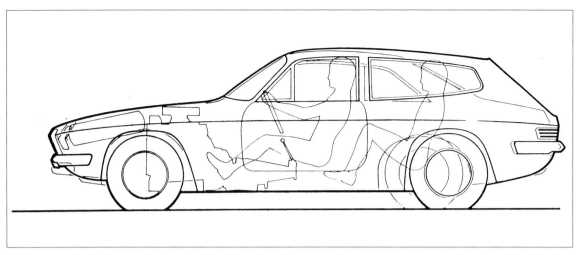

The Ogle Triplex had sown the seeds of the idea of making a sporting estate-type car on the basis of the Scimitar Coupé and capable of accommodating four people and their luggage. This outline drawing shows how the design evolved from the Coupé by extending the wheelbase slightly and placing the spare wheel ahead of the engine. Any adverse effect on the weight distribution as a result of this layout was compensated for by the position of the compact V6 engine well behind the front axle line.

This view of the prototype GTE (Grand Touring Estate) shows the original plan for the headlights was revised into a far more interesting arrangement similar to the Coupé. This example still retains the 15in Coupé slotted wheels, but the overall shape was little altered for production.

The final shape of the SE5 GTE, as it was termed, illustrates the revolutionary upswept rear wing line with contoured shoulder effect blending into the fast-back rear window line. The neat frontal appearance matched the uncluttered clean lines of the design. The wheels were equipped with GRP moulded trims to simulate alloy appearance. The doors and windscreen were carried over virtually unaltered from the Coupé, as was the bonnet and rear bumper.

The opening rear window made the GTE a very stylish estate car, and it was the first sporting car to incorporate this feature. The window in the first seventeen cars was supported by spring-loaded struts but these were replaced by gas-filled units, which were very advanced, as were the folding individual rear seats that made the car more versatile. The fascia was carried over from the Coupé, which remained in production for a couple of years after the introduction of the GTE in 1968.

This brilliant cutaway diagram by Brian Hatton illustrates perfectly the compact layout of the GTE. The short V6 engine is situated behind the front axle line allowing space for the spare wheel ahead of it and above the radiator. This leaves plenty of room below the rear luggage area for a large 17 gallon fuel tank. The perimeter design of the chassis allows the footwells to be between the chassis members so that the rear seats ahead of the rear axle will accommodate adults comfortably. The extended wheel base, compared with the Coupé, permits longer rear trailing arms locating the rear axle, which in turn gives improved geometry and larger suspension movement required for the increased loads now made possible.

This picture of a rolling GTE chassis, designed by John Crosthwaite, emphasises its robust nature and shows the excellent location of the rear axle. The long trailing links and transverse watt links ensure perfect lateral location, which endows the car with better directional stability than found with the cheaper panhard rod arrangements.

The robust wishbone front suspension seen here comprised Triumph TR6 arms and uprights, but the steering and brakes were from the Austin 1800 and Jaguar XJ6 respectively. This classic layout combined with a rigid chassis endowed the GTE with excellent handling, even if the limited suspension movement gave the car a firm ride in line with its sporting origins and performance.

This extremely clever sectioned GTE, shown at the 1968 Motor Show, was constructed by apprentices at Tamworth and reveals clearly the favourable position of the engine and seats for good weight distribution and comfort. Note also the twin roll-over bars incorporated in the pillar behind the doors which made the cabin a very safe place in which to travel.

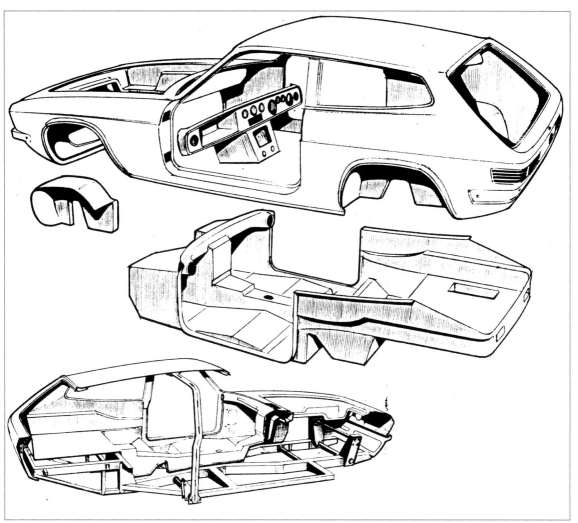

The body of the GTE consisted of two main GRP mouldings, the outer shell and the floorpan. These two massive units were then bonded together, forming an exceedingly rigid unit and adding further strength to the already stout chassis when mounted on it by twenty fixing points. Two of these attachment points were the ends of a tubular steel roll hoop behind the door apertures, which were bonded into the outer shell from the start. This made the completed car extremely safe if inverted and the impact absorption powers of the fibreglass added to the safety of the car.

Tom Scott, Reliant Sales Director, is seen on the Reliant stand at the 1968 Motor Show with Ray Wiggin, both looking very pleased with the display and probably comparing notes on the orders that flooded in at this exhibition. The public had been taken by surprise – they had not seen a car of this type before and for such a load-carrying vehicle the GTE featured many revolutionary qualities, such as individually folding rear seats and high performance.

The relatively small-scale manufacturing facility of Reliant allowed them to make changes to production models quite easily and rapidly. Thus after the first year of the model's introduction, Reliant made modifications to the GTE in response to public and media comments. These had highlighted the difficulty in filling the fuel tank and the rapidity with which the rear window became opaque in wet weather. Thus, a revised side-opening fuel cap, set at an angle, replaced the first design and a rear window wiper was introduced – another first by this innovative company.

Ogle developed the design still further and showed their concept at the Motor Show that saw the introduction of the GTE. This car differed in its headlamp arrangement, using the fashionable square units that also had shutters to cover them up in daylight. Also the roof above the front seat was a glass panel, as in the Triplex car. This car is still in the possession of the Hodge family, who owned Reliant at this period.

Three SE5 Scimitars are lined up at Portsmouth Harbour to celebrate the commissioning of HMS *Scimitar*, seen here in the background. The Navy had also co-operated previously by inviting Reliant to send some Sabres to the dockside when HMS *Sabre* was put into operation. Such publicity was always helpful.

Reliant Managing Director Ray Wiggin surveys a compound full of SE5s awaiting dispatch in 1970, when the GTE was beginning to gain a firm position in the sports-car market. His brave decision to proceed with the revolutionary Ogle design was beginning to pay off.

In October 1971 the new GTE had its first facelift. The most noticeable differences were the substitution of the four front grille slats with a one-piece chrome-cast dummy grille. At the same time the headlights were raised a few inches to comply with the latest vehicle regulations. The chrome strip along the waistline was replaced with a painted coachline and a sill polished strip added. The wheel option was now made by Dunlop, comprising a chrome-plated steel rim rivetted to a cast-alloy centre. These composite wheels have proved very difficult to restore on older cars and suffer from difficulty in balancing as they get older.

Small but significant changes were also made to the rear of the revised SE5a model, as it became known. The rear light units now incorporated the reversing lights as well and were special units for the Scimitar, subsequently employed by Aston Martin, Jensen-Healey and TVR for their models. The chrome lettering on the front and rear panels was now of a more square profile and the 'Overdrive' badge appeared on the rear of cars so equipped. The 3 litre badges on the side of the front wings were substituted by shield badges.

This photograph, taken at the 'Most Beautiful Body of the Year' contest in 1970 and introduced by BBC newsreader Richard Baker, indicates what an impact the revolutionary Ogle design had made on the fashionable world. This light-hearted display did much to help establish the Scimitar GTE as a prestigious car chosen by many show-business and influential personalities.

The BBC personality Noel Edmonds chose a Scimitar GTE as his personal transport. Apparently he was driving home to Kent in 1973 and passed the Gold Seal Car Company when he saw a GTE in the showroom and it was love at first sight! He ordered an overdrive model in Everest White there and then, fitted with electric windows and a stereo eight-track player so that he could play his favourite music on long journeys.

Following her father's use of the Triplex GTS Scimitar a few years earlier, Princess Anne expressed an interest in the GTE in 1970 and Reliant lent her an example to try. She is seen here leaving Buckingham Palace in this loan car, fitted with the GT alloy wheels which had just become optional extras on the SE5. These wheels were subsequently termed 'Princess Anne' wheels among the ownership of Scimitars and were quite highly sought after, being ½in wider than the standard steel items and more rigid yet lighter.

Clearly the trial was a success as the Queen and the Duke of Edinburgh gave Princess Anne an SE5 for Christmas in 1970. She had it finished in a characteristic dark Air Force blue with grey leather interior and registered 1420 H, in recognition of her position as Colonel-in-Chief of the 14th/20th Hussars. The car was a manual, overdrive version as opposed to the optional automatic transmission now available that was becoming more popular with lady drivers.

The make-over of the SE5 into the SE5a in 1971 affected the interior as well as the external bodywork. The most obvious difference was the fascia panel, now moulded in thermo-plastics in brown or black to match the interior trim, which could be in leather or vinyl. While the appearance was more modern, the ergonomics were not improved by the row of identical rocker switches controlling the lights, wipers etc. which could prove difficult to distinguish between in the dark. However, fresh-air ventilation and heating arrangements were marginally improved and the overall effect was more modern and well finished.

The divided rear-seat arrangement was a revolutionary feature from the introduction of the GTE and this photograph shows how versatile the layout was in practice. The carpeted backing for the rear seats made the luggage area particularly well finished and the rear seats themselves offered good leg and head room, combined with superb location aided by lap seat belts, which were a very advanced feature.

In 1975 Reliant had a particularly busy year as far as factory visits were concerned. Firstly, Mrs Thatcher, the future Prime Minister, toured the production lines and expressed great admiration for the GTE having seen how it was built. However, she claimed that shortage of cash prevented her from buying one, which sounds somewhat less than plausible.

Later in 1975 Princess Anne also toured the factory, and in particular the GTE production line, as she was about to acquire her third GTE. Her enthusiasm for the marque was obvious to all who accompanied her around the factory and her visits did much to enhance the morale of the workforce. Reliant was very busy at this time due to the undoubted success of the GTE as well as the continued demand for the three-wheelers. The royal patronage of both models no doubt contributed much to the success of Reliant at this time.

Princess Anne takes delivery of her third GTE, an SE5a model with the same registration as her previous cars. Reliant used to exchange her cars and re-paint them before re-registering them with a new number so that the cars were not identifiable as ex-royal transport. Her personal detective is holding the umbrella while Ray Wiggin is standing behind the Scimitar, and Works Director Mr Heathcote is standing in the doorway of the company office.

Scimitars were favourites of many lady drivers and particularly those with equestrian interests. Again the influence of Princess Anne is probably detectable in this trend in the 1970s. Another

Scimitars also caught the imagination of the entertainment world and such stars as David Nixon, Rita Tushingham and Hughie Jones of the Spinners were among those who chose SE5a's as their personal transport when far more expensive cars were within their reach. It says much for the style and performance of the Scimitar that it captured the appeal of many discerning owners. This scene outside the Royal Albert Hall is symptomatic of its place in the public appraisal.

factor was the Scimitar's excellent towing capability, which made it ideal for pulling horseboxes; it had a high power-to-weight ratio and short rear over-hang.

In the mid-1970s the GTE production was at its peak of about seventy cars a week and this scene of Scimitars being loaded on to a transporter must have been most satisfying to the management at Reliant. The GTE was filling a niche that no other manufacturer was satisfying and Reliant were in a position to capitalise on this situation admirably. However, it would not be long before larger car makers such as BMW, Lancia and Volvo also entered this market, with limited success.

The Scimitar was still a sports car at heart and capable of acquitting itself in competition admirably, even though it was not designed to do so. The combination of performance and handling were of a very high order in its period and here we see a perfectly standard SE5a racing at a sprint course in the Midlands, not far from its birth place, and beating far more exotic machinery such as Aston Martins and Jaguars. This car, owned and driven by me, did eighteen years of commuting, competing and towing without any modifications or special treatment, just regular servicing.

The reserves of capability built into the Scimitar chassis are evident by the performance of this super-charged, Rover V8 engined, hill-climb car built and driven by Les Trafford in the 1980s. This car eventually won its class in the Midland Hill Climb Championship against Morgans and Porsches. The body was extensively lightened but the chassis and suspension were largely unaltered, which says much for the original Crosthwaite design.

Another example of a competition-developed SE5a is this super-charged 3 litre hill-climb car built and driven by Iain Daniels of Stroud, Gloucestershire. Although of lower power than the V8 car, it eventually achieved similar times on various tracks by virtue of its even lighter weight and altered suspension geometry. Both cars had lift-off bonnet assemblies for ease of access but this did not impair the overall rigidity of the structure and gave a better weight distribution.

This photograph shows the engine and belt-driven super-charger of Iain Daniels's GTE when the lift-off front is removed. Although the radiator and some other ancillaries are non-standard, the overall layout is quite standard. The rear suspension was also standard apart from the improved dampers. Since this car is in fact road legal, although rather uncivilised, it says a lot for the original design that so much can be achieved from this inspired conception. Added to this it is very robust and rot free, in contrast to many of its contemporaries.

101

This pick-up adaptation of a damaged Scimitar by Scimpart Ltd illustrates yet again the versatility of the design made possible by the immense strength of the cruciform chassis on which the original car was based. Absolutely no additional strengthening was required in this modification and the resulting vehicle felt extremely solid and acted as an excellent tow-car for various competition models, providing ample carrying capacity, performance and comfort with undoubted style. The bodywork alteration was carried out by Terry Cox and eighteen years later the vehicle is still in fine fettle even though it has been worked hard for most of its life. What similar design could perform so well nearly thirty years after it left the factory?

The rear bumper of this late SE5a was a factory made item in fibreglass, in place of the usual chrome-plated part. Although it never appeared in production it seemed to anticipate the design of the next SE6 model, to be revealed in 1975. Also, note the inclusion of rear fog lights, also incorporated in the later SE6, ahead of its time.

CHAPTER FIVE

THE GTE EXPANDS

The revised SE6 Scimitar was introduced at the 1975 Motor Show. It was a bigger car overall by about 4in in length and width, which gave it a more square look as the original curves were stretched over the larger dimensions. The neat rubber bumper mouldings gave a much better and finished appearance as did the interior fittings appropriate to the executive market at which the car was now aimed. Naturally the SE6 was also heavier than its predecessor, which took a slight edge off the performance.

With the SE5 and SE5a models Reliant had created a niche in the market that previously had not existed, that is the sporting car estate. Others such as Volvo with their P1800 SE and Lancia with the Beta HPE tried to copy the idea but with limited success. However, this sporting car had attracted an unexpected section of the buying public in the form of the company executive who appreciated the combination of high performance with distinctive looks and handling with the capacity to carry four people. These owners also expected reasonable comfort and a degree of luxury which perhaps the first GTE lacked compared with the opposition. Hence Reliant's plan to civilise the GTE by making it slightly larger with more comfortable seats and easier to drive with the aid of optional power steering. Externally, the appearance was modernised by fitting headlights and rear fog lights in line with contemporary models. Naturally, such moves increased the weight of the resulting SE6 GTE, as it logically became known, and with the same power source the performance suffered very slightly. It still managed to acquit itself very favourably against the competition, as the following *Motor* road test figures show:

	Max. Speed (mph)	0–60mph (secs)	50–70mph in top gear (secs)	mpg
Scimitar SE6	118.3	9.6	9.9	20.7
Datsun 260Z	127	8.8	8.8	22.9
Capri Mk II 3000	117.6	9.1	5.1	20.4
MGB V8	125.3	7.7	9.0	19.8
Rover 3500	122.3	8.9	11.1	22.5

The SE6 was now in a much more critical section of the market as it was trying to be both an executive car and a sports car and consequently fell between two stools in the process. While it had the accommodation and fittings and appearance to fulfil the former role, it did not quite have the comfort and quality of equipment to truly impress. As a sports car it had lost the edge of its performance only slightly but the handling was also somewhat compromised compared with the SE5 and some of the competition. Basically, Reliant were asking an awful lot from a suspension design, particularly at the front, that dated back twenty years. While this system achieved a satisfactory compromise on the SE5 between handling and firm ride, the heavier and wider body of the SE6 taxed the design rather too much. Reliant were trying to achieve a more comfortable ride with the latest model, but the restricted suspension travel resulted in bottoming out of the springs. Higher spring rates only made the ride too firm and created body shudder as it was no longer as rigid a structure as its more compact predecessor. The designers were, however, able to offer power-assisted steering by using a modified Rover rack, which was welcomed by many prospective owners.

The chassis and bodywork did not share any parts with the SE5 and the larger doors gave rise to problems of premature dropping due to lack of strength in the hinge support panels. Thus some revisions were necessary in that area and simultaneously Reliant chose to uprate the braking system by adopting a Lockheed twin-circuit system instead of the previous Girling twin system. The revised version was termed the SE6a and was introduced in late 1976 and remained virtually unchanged in specification for the next three years.

Sales began to tail off during the late 1970s, partly due to the onset of a recession but also because the competition facing the SE6a became more intense from the cars produced by BMW and Rover, for example, who were able to develop their products to a greater extent than Reliant and so achieved higher levels of comfort and reliability. In order to expand their market share the management at Tamworth decided to investigate another niche in the car market not covered by the larger makers, and the demise of the Triumph Stag gave them the opportunity to produce a convertible version of the GTE. Ogle Design were given the opportunity to evolve a drop-head version of the GTE with minimum bodywork alteration. This objective was achieved with bodywork modification only required behind the doors after the roof was removed. The resulting GTC design looked very mature and convincing as well as being a practical four-seater with good luggage space. Theoretically, the GTC was now only in competition with the much more expensive Mercedes Benz SL range of cars, but the deepening financial depression mitigated against the success of this new model and in 1980 and 1981 rows of the new cars could be seen at the rear of the Two Gates factory awaiting buyers.

Coincidental with the introduction of the GTC, Ford adopted the Cologne-built 2.8 litre V6 engine for their range of Granada models, so Reliant had to follow suit with theirs. Thus the current GTE model with this new engine was now listed as the SE6b and the drop-head counterpart was known as the SE8b. (The SE8 was the 3 litre prototype GTC.) A certain amount of strengthening was incorporated in the new convertible GTC particularly around the scuttle area and behind the rear seats as well as linking the existing roll-over bar behind the front seats to the top of the windscreen rail, as on the Triumph Stag. The German engine had similar power to the older Essex 3 litre unit but less torque at low revs, hence the axle ratio of the 2.8 litre cars had to be lowered to compensate for this difference. Even though the smaller engine was slightly smoother it had to rev higher for the same performance as the British engine and so seemed more fussy though no less economical.

The following *Motor* road test figures make interesting comparisons:

	Max. Speed (mph)	0–60mph (secs)	50–70mph in top gear (secs)	mpg
Scimitar GTC	114.1	9.7	8.6	23.7
Triumph Stag	112.4	9.9	5.3	18.9
Mercedes 280 CE	117.9	9.5	5.7	17.2

This was not quite the last Scimitar to be produced, as Reliant eventually sold the rights to build the GTE and GTC models to a Japanese-owned company called Middlebridge, who in 1988 opened a modern factory in Beeston, Nottinghamshire, to continue production. The revised models apparently incorporated over 400 modifications but the most important of these was the use of the latest Ford 2.9 litre V6 engine with fuel injection allied to the Granada five-speed gearbox. This combination gave the new car a useful hike in performance and smoothness allied to various new luxury features. Externally, the main differences to greet the observer were the fitting of multi-spoke 6in × 15in alloy wheels, moulded body colour front and rear bumpers and larger rear-light assemblies. Interior trim was available in a variety of materials to suit customer choice with revised VDO instruments and an Italo-Volanti steering wheel, which looked totally out of place.

Greater attention to finish and customer choice was a feature of the new revitalised Scimitar and the price of roughly £23,000 placed the car in very prestigious company. Even though the Princess Royal ordered one of the new models, which she still drives, the car was too dated in many respects for the market in which it was placed and the project brought the new company into the hands of the receivers in 1990. This was partly due, it must be stated, to a legal case involving the owners of the company agreeing to buy Bentley No. 1 for a vast sum of money only to withdraw for authenticity reasons with the loss of much money. So the last remaining unfinished GTEs and factory equipment and stores were auctioned in 1990 and only seventy-seven cars were produced in this final form. Coincidentally, this is the same as the number of Sabre 6s that left the Reliant factory some seventeen years previously.

This clever contemporary Scimitar advertisement epitomises the market competition Reliant was now pitting the SE6 against. It features Triumph, BMW, Rover and Jaguar models and the GTE certainly was able to compete in the showroom, but aspects of its ride and reliability did not always compare favourably. However, the SE6 sold well for several years and proved profitable.

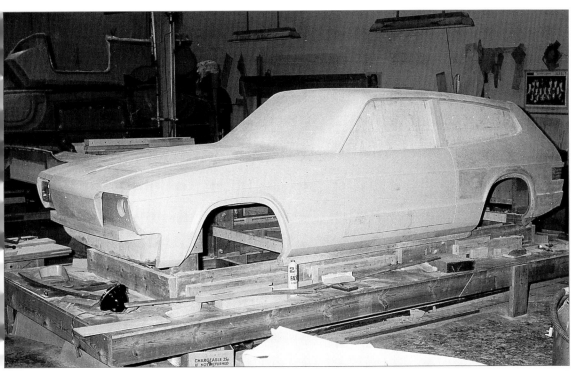

In order to develop the revised GTE the body development team under Ken Wood literally cut an SE5 bodyshell longitudinally down the middle and inserted a 4 in section of fibreglass in the gap and then did the same across the car, ahead of the B-pillar. The resultant dimensions defined the shape of the new car which looked very similar to the existing SE5 but did not in fact share one body panel. This was not a particular problem as new moulds were needed anyway and costings were much the same whether or not modifications were made. The front moulding was changed more radically with a separate lower bumper section and larger outer headlamps. Rather more expensive from the development aspect was that all the glass had to be re-specified, as well as the bright trim.

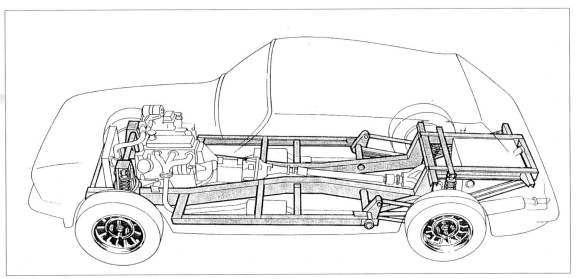

The chassis frame of the new SE6 had to be lengthened and widened to match the revised bodyshell, but still conformed to the excellent basic design devised by ex-BRM designer John Crosthwaite. An extra cross-member was added under each front seat, to which the latter was bolted. The position of the compact engine and gearbox behind the front axle line contributed to an excellent weight distribution. The larger fuel tank now held 20 gallons of fuel.

The new front of the SE6, as it was logically termed, now featured a black plastic dummy grille and black rubber bumper coverings with a minimum of bright trim confined to the anodised aluminium upper rim of the bumpers and grille in line with current fashion. The headlamp arrangement was certainly welcome as the SE5 was deficient in this area.

The rear rubber bumper was in fact identical to the front moulding, which was an expedient piece of design considering the cost of tooling for such an item. Ironically the bright aluminium trims were not the same as the front. In line with contemporary practice rear fog lamps were now built in to the rear valance in parallel with the front indicator units. Again, this whole assembly was bolted on to the main bodyshell, rendering replacement as a result of damage simpler.

The overall design of the new SE6, still the work of Ogle Design, gave the impression of a much more mature and well-finished car. The bumpers blended in with the bodywork extremely well and the new swage lines on the bonnet and waist emphasised the solidity of the shape. Although the Dunlop chrome alloy wheels were carried over from the SE5a, to some the purity of the original SE5 was somewhat lost and the subtle curves had become more square, particularly at the front. However, the car gained authority from the changes.

All the novel features of the SE5 were retained at the rear of the SE6, including the rear-window wiper and the new central fuel filler – very convenient at petrol stations where it mattered on which side of the pumps you stopped. The new rubber bumpers were beneficial if the car became involved in small collisions or scrapes as it usually rebounded unharmed. Naturally the carrying capacity of the new car was also greater as a result of its increased width and length, enhanced by the larger rear-opening hatch for loading purposes. The fuel tank was now 20 gallons capacity, giving a possible range of 500 miles.

The instrument panel was more modern in appearance than the SE5 but contained no more instruments than the earlier model. However, extra features did include remote-control door mirrors and rear fog lights. As on the SE5, electric windows were optional but most other equipment was standard. A sliding, folding sunshine roof by Tudor Webasto was a dealer-fitted option. Transmission was either a four-speed manual with overdrive gearbox, or a three-speed automatic Ford gearbox.

The interior of the SE6 was remodelled to an even greater degree than the exterior. The seats were now far more luxurious with cloth facings or leather options, featuring rather quaint button-back designs. The greater width made the rear seat capable of accommodating two adults or three children, which was quite an achievement for a sporting car. Seat belts were fitted all round, ahead of most of its competitors, and the larger dimensions enabled even more luggage to be carried, particularly if the rear seats were folded flat.

Here we see the two main body moulds being produced simultaneously before being bonded together on the huge jig. During this bonding process the combined shell was bolted to its chassis to ensure correct alignment. All the fibreglass mouldings were laid up by hand by saturating sheets of glassfibre matt with polyester resin in layers, whose number varied according to the strength required in critical areas of the shell.

The finished bodyshells were left outside to cure while mounted on the chassis, which could take several days. The slower the curing process the less surface distortion occurred. When the SE5a was being produced there was great pressure on the moulding shop so that the bodyshells were cured in heated ovens to hasten the process. This forced process led to ripples in the surface of the bodywork, which is often seen on cars produced during 1975 and 1976, when production was at its peak.

On reaching the assembly area on trollies, the bodies were lifted off their chassis to enable the major mechanical components to be fitted, such as engines, gearboxes, axles and fuel tanks. The bodies were then lowered back on to the corresponding chassis, having travelled aloft while these major units were fitted.

While the bodies were separated from the chassis the doors and electric wiring looms were fitted, since these items were far more accessible in the absence of the chassis and running gear. This rather cumbersome assembly operation did ensure that each body fitted its chassis accurately and the quality of build was far ahead of other specialist manufacturers, even if it did not quite approach that of the larger executive car makers, such as BMW and Mercedes, which Reliant were now aiming to match.

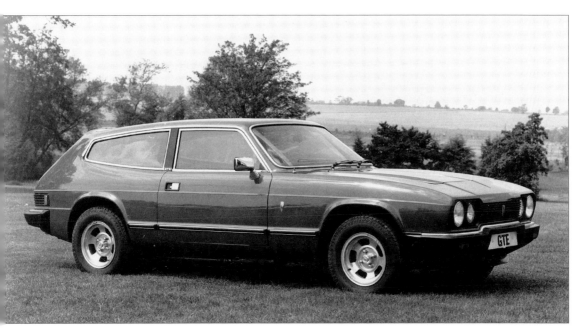

In 1980 Ford abandoned the 3 litre Essex V6 engine in favour of the German built 2.8 V6 Cologne unit. Reliant naturally had to follow suit and quickly adapted the chassis mountings to accommodate the new lighter engine. They retained the overdrive gearbox, dating back to the Zodiac Mk III of 1963, by using a South African Transit bell-housing which happened to use the same combination of engine and gearbox.

Only slight modifications were made to the bodywork to distinguish the new SE6b from its predecessors. These consisted of a deeper black plastic dummy grille at the front, incorporating a larger shield badge in the centre, and abandoning the polished letter bar above the previous narrow grille. Also, black and chrome rubbing strips were added to the sides of the bodywork between the wheel arches, which gave the impression of greater length as well as some protection. Steel wheels with GRP covers were still standard fare but Wolfrace alloy wheels were usually specified by purchasers.

The SE6 was really an enlargement and refinement of the original SE5 theme and Ray Wiggin was eager to explore the future bodystyles to maintain the success of the marque. Logically he consulted Ogle Design to suggest the new direction for the Scimitar, which would have the title SE7, and one such radical new thought is seen here.

Wiggin also pondered on the possibility of a four-door GTE and Ogle very cleverly adapted his earlier SE6 shape to accommodate a pair of rear doors without losing the identity of the established Scimitar. However, Reliant now had new owners, the Nash family, which resulted in the resignation of Ray Wiggin in 1977 and the Ogle plans for an SE7 were ditched. Ten years later Reliant also suspended production of the SE6b.

One exciting variation on the SE6 theme was pursued with the aid of Ogle Design in the form of a convertible. This was first conceived in late 1978, based on a 3 litre chassis and termed the SE8. No changes were made from the front of the bodywork to the back of the passenger doors. Thereafter the rear wing line was remodelled to form a boot section and an additional brace, from the roll-over hoop to the reinforced windscreen frame, similar to the Triumph Stag.

The light-coloured area at the rear of the body section of this car shows the revised fibreglass section, which has been bonded on to the unchanged front of a cut-down GTE bodyshell. A mock-up of the hood shape is in place for assessment. Only one bodyshell was worked on for this project as fibreglass is such an ideal medium with which to develop a bodyshape. It can be cut back or added to very easily until the designers and managers are satisfied with the final shape from which a master mould can then be taken for production purposes.

Additional bracing was incorporated into the scuttle area of the moulded shell which extended up the windscreen pillars to meet the central brace from the roll-over bar. This did much to reduce the scuttle-shake as well as offering considerable protection in the case of involuntary inversion. All the metal bracing was bonded into the main shell which added further strength as well as hiding and protecting the metal work from corrosion.

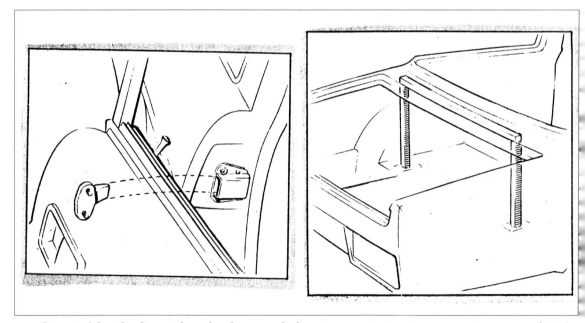

In order to stabilise the doors, when closed, against body movement, an extra tongue was incorporated in the latch area thus removing any strain from the door lock itself. Additional bracing was also built into the area between the rear seats and boot, which hardly intruded into the load space and acted as a support for the removable front panel thus allowing long items such as golf clubs to be accommodated.

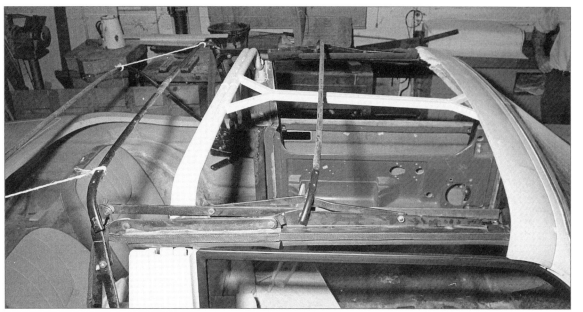

This photograph, taken during development of the new convertible to be known as the GTC, shows clearly the bracing structure and roll-over twin hoops. The soft-top framework is being evolved at this stage and a Triumph Stag assembly was used as a basis for the design. This was then modified to fit the dimensions of the Scimitar, which was slightly wider.

Here we can see the finished bodyshell with the bracing structure fully incorporated into the fibreglass shell and finished off to a high standard with upholstery and fittings. The seating arrangements were unaltered during this conversion and so the GTC was a full four-seater with exactly the same passenger room as its GTE predecessor. The doors and screen surrounds are no longer chrome trim but, in line with the contemporary fashion, are black.

The GTC was eventually termed the SE8b, as opposed to the corresponding GTE being the SE6b, now that both models were fitted with the Cologne-built 2.8 litre Ford V6 engine. However, the prototype GTC was still fitted with a 3 litre Essex engine and was sold to motoring journalist Mike McCarthy, who used it for many years. That car now tows ERAs and racing D-type Jaguars for its present owner. The frontal appearance of the GTC and GTE was identical and differed from the 3 litre models only in the grille, which was a deeper plastic moulding with the large shield badge in the centre rather than on the bodywork above the grille. The name Scimitar no longer appeared on the front of the car.

The rear aspect of the GTC was profoundly different as a result of the conversion to drop-head format. The rubber bumper mouldings and the rear light assemblies were unchanged from the GTE model, as was the fuel filler cap. The boot lid blended in well with the rear bodywork, incorporating a slight lip which added a finishing touch to the rear end. On this pre-production car the self-adhesive badging, which can be seen on production cars, is missing from the lower lip of the boot lid.

This rare scene in the very small production area allotted to the Scimitars in the 1980s shows a GTC bodyshell about to be re-united with its chassis, now that all the running gear has been fitted to it. Note that the chassis frame is galvanised, as were all Reliant chassis at this time, which allied to the rot-proof bodywork accorded the car the prospect of being a very long-lived machine.

The finished GTC looks particularly handsome in white and even in the snowy conditions such as these it proved to be a reasonably cosy car to travel in. The polished Wolfrace wheels were an optional fitting but most cars left the factory with them as they were considered very desirable at that time. Note that a moulded waistline rubbing strip now adhered to the lower flanks of the Scimitar, helping to give the car a lower appearance as well as offering some protection to the bodywork.

The fascia of the GTC differed from the GTE only in minor details, such as the steering-wheel rubber boss and the absence of a rear wiper/washer control at the bottom left of the central console. This example is clearly an automatic, as were over half the production models at this stage. It is also fully equipped with electric mirrors, controlled by the switches above the heater controls, and virtually all the cars had electric windows and even a heated rear window in the optional hard-top.

The seating arrangement was identical in both models, with the option of nylon cloth or leather trim materials. The curious choice of button-back upholstery is very unusual in the automobile world and was criticised by some journalists at the time. The backs of the rear seat folded down as they had in the GTE, offering excellent luggage capacity through to the boot, which had a removable panel separating it from the passenger bay. The hood folded down behind the rear seats without intruding on passenger space, although this naturally limited luggage capacity.

So many attractive convertibles lose a lot of their appeal when their hoods are erected but that cannot be said of the GTC which is possibly more handsome when the hood is raised. Furthermore, the generous window area of the hood made the interior far less claustrophobic than many drop-heads as well as adding to the visual balance of the profile view.

This rear aspect of the GTC emphasises the unusually large window area built into the design of the hood as well as its neat fit. The full badge lettering is apparent on this production model. The manner in which the rear bumper apron extends fully to the rear wheel arch differs from the GTE, as do the rear light surrounds which now lack air vents on the corners.

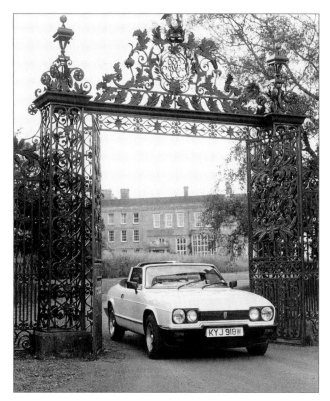

The first convertible Reliant since 1963, and the first drop-head Scimitar ever, made its entry on to the motoring scene in 1980 and a very imposing machine it looked. It was poised to fill the gap in the market left by the demise of the Triumph Stag. The formula of a full four-seater, large-engined convertible was fairly unusual at this period with only Mercedes offering a similar vehicle.

The optional hard-top was a very substantial moulding requiring two people to fit it. However, the effort was worth it in winter conditions as it was particularly snug with good sound insulation and generous window area. The rear window was even heated. The external appearance was even more attractive than when the hood was raised, which is not perhaps surprising, but it made the car a very smart fixed-head coupé with very up-to-date styling. The bright trims on the bumpers and the Wolfrace wheels gave it an air of quality, which compared well with the more prestigious marques.

The royal association with Scimitars was maintained by the use, albeit briefly, of a GTC by Prince Edward, seen here in Windsor Great Park with an unknown passenger. His elder sister remained loyal to the GTE, although it is perhaps surprising that the GTC did not take her fancy when it was introduced. It was very popular with lady owners at the time.

The GTC brought a touch of added glamour to the Scimitar range in the early 1980s, just as a recession was about to begin. But it was not enough to make the car a sales success, only 422 cars were built and many of these stayed in the showroom for extended periods, or in the parking lot behind the Tamworth factory. The economic climate and the lack of future development meant the end for the Scimitar GTE and GTC models. In 1986 Reliant closed down the production line and eventually sold off part of the factory.

The boot area of the GTC was quite reasonable and very usable, especially when the detachable front carpeted panel was removed. In addition, with the hood raised and the rear seats folded down a considerable amount of luggage could be carried. The boot was also capable of taking the golf clubs and skis that are so often mentioned as the measure of a car's luggage capacity in the brochures aimed at the executive section of the market, where the Scimitar hoped to reside.

Ritchie Spencer, a member of the Nash family, became the new Managing Director of Reliant and he chose to consult the prestigious Italian designer Bertone for a possible successor to the Ogle-designed GTE. One proposal was produced by Bertone in 1982 and did progress to the prototype stage, seen here in the development department of Reliant. This rolling shell was intended to be fitted with a Rover 3.5 litre V8 engine and was a most elegant looking vehicle. Known as the SE82 in the department, it sadly never progressed beyond this stage and was tragically cut up by those who had built it and so ended the line of the GTE as far as Reliant were concerned. Production of the 2.8 litre version continued at a trickle until 1986 when the plant was gutted and eventually sold.

The Middlebridge GTE adopted the latest Ford V6 2.9 fuel-injection Scorpio engine and five-speed gearbox which endowed the revised GTE with a notably improved performance. The suspension was fitted with tailor-made Bilstein shock absorbers and a rear anti-roll bar, which offered improved handling, as one would expect. Wheel size was also increased to 15in diameter with appropriate lower profile tyres improving appearance and grip. The basic suspension geometry was unaltered which says a great deal for a twenty-year-old design.

Interior changes were mainly cosmetic as a greater range of trim materials were on offer, but the only additional equipment was central locking in an attempt to keep up with the current executive car market at which this car was really aimed. As its sports car origins gradually faded, despite its improved performance, Princess Anne was offered one of the earliest production models to try and she subsequently decided to replace her last Reliant-built GTE with a Middlebridge version in 1988. She still runs that car to this day.

A number of outside consortia showed interest in continuing production of the GTE, but the only one able to finance the initiative was the Middlebridge Group, owned by the Japanese industrialist Mr Nakauchi. The company succeeded in acquiring the rights to the GTE name for £400,000 in 1987. They established a small modern factory unit in Beeston, Nottingham, and

commenced production initially from kits of parts retained by Reliant for this very purpose. Allegedly Middlebridge made 450 alterations to their version, but from the outside the only obvious ones were realigned rear exhaust pipes, new rear lights and modified front and rear bumper trims.

The factory unit in Nottingham, where Middlebridge built the GTE, was extremely well equipped with sophisticated chassis-alignment jigs and spraying booths which enabled them to turn out a very well-finished car. Unfortunately, the company was over ambitious in terms of potential output and sales and this eventually resulted in financial disaster, admittedly influenced by the company's external dealings with a certain vintage Bentley. In 1990 the company was finally wound up with a closing auction of the final unfinished car assembly plant and spare parts.

The prototype Middlebridge GTE was purchased by Dan Mitchell from Warwickshire and is seen here when new. Dan still owns the car which has proved very enjoyable and reliable. The design certainly deserved to live on with suitable mechanical and equipment improvements. Inevitably, finance and fantasy determine the destiny of such projects which really needed the backing of much larger organisations capable of the development required alongside more established products. In total only seventy-seven Middlebridge GTEs were made.

CHAPTER SIX

RETURN OF THE TWO-SEATER

When Reliant decided wisely to return to the small sports-car market, left wide open by the demise of the MGB and TR7, their Managing Director, Ritchie Spencer, consulted Italian designers for proposals on bodywork. Michelotti's submission was chosen even though it had apparently already been turned down by Triumph (he had designed many Triumph models in the past). The frontal aspect of the design was bland but reasonably modern and inoffensive, but the choice of a title, SS1, was hardly inspiring and had unfortunate war-time connotations. Sadly, any suggestion of commissioning proposals from British designers, such as Tony Stevens and Ogle Design, were not approved.

In the mid-1980s Reliant reverted to the idea of producing a no-nonsense two-seater sports car reminiscent of the Sabre 4 in 1961. The main manufacturers, particularly BMC, were abandoning this sector of the market due to the punitive safety regulations being imposed by the American authorities. Reliant, however, were never able to or interested in selling cars to the USA but could see that the UK market was now starved of sports cars, except for the exclusive Morgan at one extreme and flimsy kit cars at the other. The opportunity for Reliant to enter this market could not have been more timely with the demise of interest in the larger and more expensive GTE/GTC models. Alas, as we shall see, this opportunity was largely wasted through lack of imagination and judgement regarding the shape of the new car and finally the complicated and expensive manner in which they chose to produce it.

Suggestions for possible Reliant-based sports cars had already been made to Reliant by designers such as Tony Stevens with his Sienna and Cipher designs but these ideas were rejected, apparently for cost reasons. Ritchie Spencer, the new Managing Director of Reliant since 1977, decided that only the Italians could design sports cars and opted for a Michelotti proposal which, rumour has it, Triumph had previously rejected. This same designer had, of course, produced some very successful designs for Triumph in the form of the Herald, Spitfire, TR4, 1300, 2000 and Stag.

Not content with utilising any chassis components or running gear from the small car range of four-wheelers, Reliant chose to start with a clean sheet of paper. Their Engineering Director, Ed Osmond, devised a very clever semi-space frame chassis formed by steel pressings and a central backbone surrounding the transmission to the rear differential. All-independent suspension was incorporated using Vauxhall Chevette front wishbones with horizontal front dampers, while special trailing arms supported the rear wheels linked to a Ford Sierra chassis-mounted differential. Even though Reliant had, up to this time, produced all the chassis for their cars themselves, inexplicably they chose to have the new sports car's chassis frame made in Germany, and to complete the ill-conceived picture they called the car the Scimitar SS1. One might have thought the reason for the removal of a similar title given to early Jaguars due to wartime activities would have dawned on Reliant too. Not content with having the chassis of the new car made by outside suppliers, parts of the bodywork were also contracted out to Dunlop, who produced the flexible front and rear bumpers as well as the wings. These were also pliable to absorb minimal impacts. The consequence of all this scattered production was that the assembly operators at Reliant were faced with the huge task of making all these various components fit satisfactorily with the tolerances allowed for the individual panels. It is difficult to understand why the management did not follow the precedent of the previous fifty years and produce both chassis and bodywork in-house with facilities which had now been released with the demise of the GTE/GTC lines.

The choice of Ford engines was logical, together with gearboxes and rear transmission to match, but the need for both 1300cc and 1600cc versions was mystifying as the former was hardly capable of producing a sporting performance. The resulting SS1 did in fact handle very well and in 1600cc guise had adequate performance but it met with a lukewarm response from the press and enthusiasts by virtue of its controversial appearance. From the driver's point of view, the instruments from a Metro did not improve the vehicle.

In comparison with the few open two-seaters still available the SS1 was competitive in performance and economy and price as the *Motor* road test figures testify:

	Price (£)	Max. Speed (mph)	0–60mph (secs)	30–50mph in fourth gear (secs)	mpg
SS1 1600cc	7,795	105.3	10.5	9.1	26.5
Fiat X1/9	7,500	107.7	9.9	7.4	29.0
Morgan 4/4	9,300	103.0	10.0	9.3	29.3

The 1300cc version, about £1,000 cheaper than the 1600cc car, had fairly leisurely performance, although no magazine road-test figures were ever published, and sales reflected the lack of desirability of this model.

Reliant had estimated that sales of sports cars in this sector of the market in the UK were about 7,500 per annum and that they should achieve a reasonable percentage of this annual total in view of the declining number of models still in production. However, after two years Reliant had sold less than 1,000 cars of either capacity and this was not a viable quantity. They were contracted to take far more chassis from their German supplier than this, which added to their embarrassment. At this point they rather belatedly decided to have these chassis galvanised in line with the policy that had been introduced some years earlier on the three-wheeler range as well as the GTE/GTC range. This factor has subsequently led to severe chassis corrosion problems for these early cars as the gauge of steel used in the design of the clever chassis was far thinner than in the other Reliant cars, which lasted well enough without galvanisation because of their robust construction.

The extra protection afforded by galvanising the chassis was not doubt a good sales feature but an even more persuasive one was the introduction of a Nissan 1800cc turbo-charged model known as the 1800ti. This transformed the car into an extremely quick sports model capable of matching any of the competition. As well as holding the road equally well, due to its relatively sophisticated chassis, it had the prospect of a long life thanks to the well-protected chassis and durable bodywork. Unfortunately, Reliant did little to uprate the appearance of the model apart from a black rubber spoiler screwed to the boot lid and the addition of wider alloy wheels as standard. The following figures recorded by *Motor* magazine indicate the improvement achieved by adopting this new engine:

	Price (£)	Max. Speed (mph)	0–60mph (secs)	30–50mph in fourth gear (secs)	mpg
Scimitar 1800ti	9,750	128.2	6.8	5.4	24.9
Morgan Plus 4	11,550	111.3	9.0	6.8	25.7
Panther 2.8	9,850	110.9	7.9	6.6	22.8

However, despite this scintillating performance, sales still did not accelerate in the same way as the car performed on the road and its styling must have been the main cause, for owners will tolerate lack of quality and even reliability if the car they drive is a source of admiration and even envy. This clearly was not the case with the

SS1 and Reliant eventually realised this when it turned to William Towns to clean up the body style to improve its appeal. His first attempt was the SS2 which was shown to the media at the time when an American concern, Universal Motors, expressed interest in promoting the car in the USA. Only a prototype was ever produced of this version but an evolutionary shape derived from the SS2 was adopted by Reliant in 1989, and was known as the SST in recognition of Towns' input. Sensibly, Reliant decided once again to make the whole bodywork in-house from fibreglass, using a smaller number of individual panels and hence improving the fit and finish of the final product. While the SST was a far neater looking car with fewer panels and creases, it still appeared rather bland because the overall shape remained unaltered.

The sleeker appearance and better finish were the result of the body being composed of just two large mouldings, the whole front of the car including the engine compartment in one, and the rear bulkhead, wings and rear panel part of the other. The only components retained from the previous model were the bonnet and boot lid. Mechanically, there were few changes apart from adopting the latest 1400cc Ford engine in place of the 1300 and 1600 pair. The new car was shown at the 1989 Motorfair and production proceeded on a basis of dealer orders due to the financial instability of Reliant, which was caused by the management's property speculation.

Eventually Reliant went into receivership in 1991. They were rescued by their component suppliers, Beans Industries, who made a Beans car between the world wars. This was a logical move by Beans as Reliant owed then considerable sums for essential castings and forgings used in the three-wheelers, which were still the mainstay of the company. At this point Beans re-introduced the name Sabre and uprated the SST further by adding side skirts and rear spoilers to the two-seater. This refurbishment made the car more modern in appearance, if somewhat fussy. In late 1993 Beans decided to rationalise the engine supply for the Sabre by replacing both the Ford 1400 and Nissan 1800 units with Rover K-series 1.4 and 2.0 twin-cam engines. The performance naturally fell between that of the previous cars, with a top speed of about 120mph and a 0–60mph figure of 9.4 seconds and 8 seconds respectively. At last this was an all-British car but the price tag was now £14,000, which was still £4,000 cheaper than the nearest competitor in the shape of the Mazda MX5.

Beans ownership of Reliant was only to last another year before they too went into receivership and in 1994 a consortium called Avonex took control. Meanwhile, the Scimitar Sabre trickled out of Tamworth until 1995 when these latest owners ran into financial trouble and Reliant really looked doomed to disappear altogether. However, the three-wheelers were still in demand and Kevin Leach, who was based in the Channel Islands, took over the ailing company and put Jonathan Heynes in charge. Despite intentions of re-establishing the sports car side of the business, no more Sabres emerged from Reliant after 1995 and production was focused on the original three-wheelers. About 2,200 SS1/SST/Sabres were produced in total and the prospect of any more Reliant sports cars now looks remote.

The chassis of the new SS1 was a complex unit based on a pressed steel backbone with semi-space frame outriggers to support the body in the required places. It was designed by Ed Osmond, Director of Engineering at Reliant and previously employed by Triumph. The structure proved very rigid and light but quite difficult to make and the contract for its manufacture was given to a German company. This move was contrary to Reliant's previous policy of producing as much of their cars in-house as possible and was curious since they had a very competent chassis-building department to produce the three-wheeler chassis and the extra capacity now that the GTE was being discontinued.

This cutaway diagram illustrates the layout of the suspension quite clearly. At the front the wishbones were derived from the Vauxhall Chevette, but the top one was modified to activate the transverse inboard telescopic dampers. It was a clever design to keep suspension loads close to the centre of the chassis, but the top wishbones were subject to some failures after many years of service. The rear suspension was fabricated by trailing arms and coil-spring damper units with a Ford Sierra differential mounted on the chassis. This in turn was driven by a Ford 1300 or 1600cc CVH unit and five-speed gearbox.

The Michelotti design was very reminiscent of the TR7 shape, even though the latter was a Harris Mann conception. The wedge shape was the current fashion but the multitude of creases, some of which concealed shut-lines and panel gaps, made the profile of the SS1 particularly fussy. The flares on the front and rear wheel arches did not blend very happily with the other body lines and gave rise to much press criticism at the time.

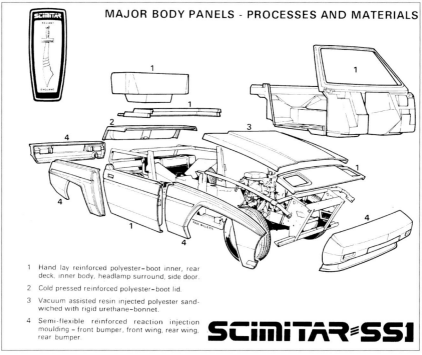

MAJOR BODY PANELS - PROCESSES AND MATERIALS

1 Hand lay reinforced polyester–boot inner, rear deck, inner body, headlamp surround, side door.

2 Cold pressed reinforced polyester–boot lid.

3 Vacuum assisted resin injected polyester sandwiched with rigid urethane–bonnet.

4 Semi-flexible reinforced reaction injection moulding – front bumper, front wing, rear wing, rear bumper.

SCIMITAR SS1

The body panels were all bolted to the main chassis structure, which made potential repair easier and cheaper, but they proved to be a headache during production as a result of the different materials from which these panels were made and the corresponding different tolerances during their manufacture. The only parts made by Reliant were the central passenger cell, doors, boot well and lid. They also made the bonnet but by a different process. Dunlop provided the flexible front, side and rear panels, which seemed to create the most problems during assembly. Why Reliant, with all its GRP expertise, chose not to make all the bodywork itself is a complete mystery.

The pop-up headlamps, derived from TR7 units, allowed the bonnet line to offer little wind resistance but could cause problems in service when only one operated due to electrical problems, not uncommon in fibreglass-bodied cars. The front nose cone and wings were moulded from a rubberised deformable plastic which resisted minor impacts. However, with ageing these panels tended to crack instead, thus reducing their initial cost-saving benefit when replacements were required.

In common with the front panel, the rear unit was also rubberised to absorb minor collisions in the place of conventional bumpers. The rear lights originated from the British Leyland parts bin, as did the front headlights which were common to Metro vans. The wrap-over design of the boot lid was similar to the Scimitar Coupé and prevented the ingress of water into the boot whatever the condition of the seals and even when opened in the wet.

The instrument panel will be recognisable as derived from the Metro, as were the headlamps, front discs and switchgear. The seats are from the same manufacturer, only the TR7 model in this case. The driving position was very good even if the ambience was rather bland and saloon-like in appearance. The gear change was very positive, as one would expect from a Ford five-speed unit, and the SS1 driving experience was a revelation considering its less than impressive appearance.

The chassis of the SS1 was probably its most impressive feature, except for the fact that being made from steel it was prone to corrosion. To address this problem after chassis number 900 all chassis were galvanised, in line with the later GTE/GTC and three-wheeler models. Even more important, however, was the adoption of the Nissan 1800cc turbo-charged engine, for the additional model known as the 1800ti. Apart from strengthening the rear differential mounting, no chassis alterations accompanied this change and the design was fully capable of handling the extra power now available. This model was way ahead of its class in terms of performance, and was capable of reaching 130mph. The only means of external identification was the presence of a new badge on the boot lid and a plastic spoiler attached to the same panel.

Reliant produced LHD versions of all their sports cars, mainly for the Benelux market, where the marque had a small but loyal following. Here we see a LHD 1800ti fitted with an optional hardtop. The wide variation of panel gaps is very evident on this early car which was much improved on the SST.

The SS1 has been used for sprinting and racing by members of the Sabre and Scimitar Owners Club. The 1800ti version is particularly competitive especially when modified in both engine and chassis departments, as this example sponsored by Graham Walker Ltd has demonstrated to good effect.

An optional hard-top was eventually offered for winter use and when fitted improved the profile considerably, as well as the interior comfort in poor weather. As with the GTC, a heated rear window was incorporated and subsequently this feature was much sought after by owners of early cars. These early models also suffered from the lack of a galvanised chassis and after about ten years replacement chassis were being fitted to less well-maintained cars due to extensive corrosion of the thin pressed-steel structure.

William Towns is a British designer with some fine cars to his credit, most notably the Aston Martin DBS and V8 derivatives. He was commissioned by Reliant to restyle the SS1, possibly for launching it in the USA market, and so the SS2 seen here was conceived. The basic central structure was retained but all the external panels were re-modelled, eliminating the numerous creases and shut-lines of the SS1, as well as the retracting headlamps, to produce a much smoother effect that was altogether more appealing. Unfortunately, such a radical development was not put into production, probably for cost reasons, and the only prototype was built by Towns.

Reliant, however, adopted some of the SS2's features when revising the SS1 to produce the SST, the 'T' being in recognition of Towns' original input. The new body was now designed to be made entirely of fibreglass at the Tamworth factory, as it should always have been. Apart from using fewer mouldings, which fitted together more accurately, they achieved better water and noise intrusion in use and must have made savings in unit costs, apart from the original mould production. The result was a much more acceptable shape, even if somewhat bland, and was only let down by the rather blunt and plain rear end which was slightly relieved by the fitment of a boot spoiler on the 1800ti models.

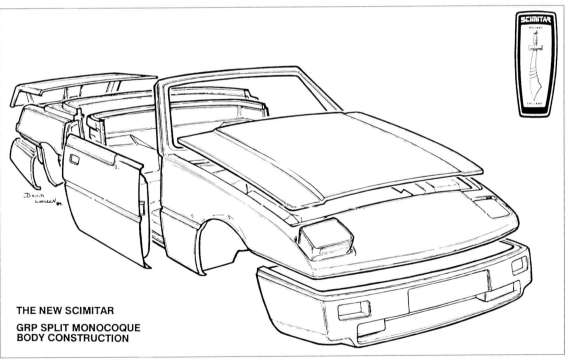

THE NEW SCIMITAR

**GRP SPLIT MONOCOQUE
BODY CONSTRUCTION**

The new SST bodywork was called a split monocoque, and comprised far fewer separate panels than the SS1 and was now made entirely of fibreglass at Tamworth. Only the bonnet and boot-lid mouldings were common to the earlier model. Mechanically there were no changes initially, but later the Ford 1400cc engine replaced the 1300cc version. The interior was basically unaltered apart from the addition of some strips of wood veneer on the 1800ti. Even though the separate bumper mouldings were no longer made of a flexible material, their replacement in cases of accidental damage was relatively easy and inexpensive.

The rear view of the SST was probably its weakest feature, looking rather heavy and droopy due to the low position of the light units and emphasised on this model by the large darker bumper moulding. The erected hood suits the bodyshape and was well made. If a little fiddly to stow away, it could be raised quickly and the large rear window made the car reasonably light inside when the hood was up.

The SST in profile did not look unlike the Triumph TR7, whose retractable headlamp mechanisms and seats it shared. The finish and shut-lines of the bodywork were far superior to those of the SS1, since Reliant now made the complete structure from large GRP mouldings ensuring consistent panel dimensions and gaps. The boot lid and bonnet were the only panels in common with the earlier model.

This under-bonnet photograph shows the installation of the Nissan 1800 turbo unit which was very compact. Note the position of the spare wheel ahead of the engine, as on the GTE models, which rendered it quite difficult to remove, although it released more room in the boot where most spare wheels are kept. It was also a good safety feature for absorbing frontal impacts. In this SST model it is apparent that the whole front bodywork is one moulding, without separate wings, making for a very rigid and neat construction.

Following a period in receivership, Reliant was purchased by Beans Industries, who for many years were suppliers of basic engine and suspension castings for most of the cars produced at Tamworth. In an attempt to revitalise sales of the small sports car, a further revision of the bodywork was undertaken, largely involving the front valance moulding incorporating the air intake, and lower sill moulding below the doors. The earlier sports car name of Sabre was now revived so that these latest models were rather clumsily called Scimitar Sabres. In 1995 a final change was introduced to the mechanical specification and Rover 1.4 and 2.0 litre engines were fitted, with appropriate gearboxes, and were presented at the Motor Show.

This final version of the Scimitar Sabre was the swansong of Reliant sports cars but it was at last an impressive and neat-looking car some ten years after its inception. Sadly, the competition had overtaken the car by this time in the form of the Mazda MX5 in particular, and the sales figures as well as the financial situation at Reliant spelled the end to sports-car production at Tamworth for ever.

The rear of the last Scimitar Sabre is perhaps a fitting view of this range of cars which lacked nothing in terms of performance and handling, so important for a sports car. However, the early resistance to its appearance and build quality was something the model could never quite escape from and rather like its earlier namesake from the 1960s it was never able to fulfil its true potential, although perhaps for different reasons, but controversial styling was the main one.

CHAPTER SEVEN

RELIANT-BASED PROJECTS

The projects featured in this section are all powered by the Reliant alloy OHV engine, seen here. This engine, derived from the pre-war Austin 7 unit, has been the backbone of the economy range of Reliant vehicles since the Second World War and is still in production. The alloy cased gearbox, together with the rear axle, is also produced in-house and the combination has proved very efficient and long-lived.

From the very beginning of Reliant Engineering to the present day all Reliant vehicles have been based on separate chassis and body construction, the latter being moulded from fibreglass since 1956. Such a method of making cars presents the opportunity for outside designers and body-builders to construct their own versions of models, based on the chassis and running gear of the basic production car. Until the late 1950s Reliant only made three-wheeled vehicles, which had little potential for the special builder, but with the introduction of the Rebel and later Kitten four-wheeled economy cars the situation changed. Reliant models offered the additional attraction of being made totally within one factory, including the engines, gearboxes and axles. This was the ideal environment for freelance designers, such as Tony Stevens, to construct their projects in.

At this time, Tony Stevens was under pressure from colleagues to produce an entirely new British sports car and hence the availability of a developed chassis with existing running gear, which was only to be found at Reliant in the shape of the Kitten saloon, was ideal. In order to get financial backing from banks he had to prove that a market existed for such a project. The demise of the soon to be dropped MGB and TR7 models was not the sort of message that impressed the financial institutions. Only Morgan appeared to be successful in their eyes, having a six- to seven-year waiting list, so Stevens opted for a traditional Morgan-like design in order to satisfy his backers that such a project was likely to be viable. Only one car was ever made and it was featured in the July 1977 issue of *Autocar* magazine. This car still exists and is owned by the designer's son.

Stevens' next design, the Cipher, was an up to the minute concept, again based on Reliant running gear but sufficiently modified to fit the more modern layout. This time Stevens obtained backing from Grundy, the stainless exhaust company. When Reliant built two of the Ciphers themselves they reported to Stevens, and hence to Grundy, that it would require a vast sum of money to make the Cipher a production possibility. However, it is likely that Reliant hoped Grundy would be so keen to proceed that they would put up this sort of backing and possibly buy into Reliant itself on the basis of its certain success. Grundy had no intention of providing such a level of support and were surprised, as indeed was Stevens, at Reliant's assessment of the project. This resulted in the withdrawal of Grundy's interest and in turn Reliant could hardly go ahead, given their earlier verdict.

There is little doubt that the Cipher could have been produced by Reliant on a commercially viable basis and that it would have been a success. This is emphasised by the number of MX5 models, which followed a very similar body design and were in an even higher price bracket than the Cipher would have been, that were sold in the UK and around the world. Tony Stevens firmly believes that potentially 20,000 a year could have been sold, which would indeed have made 'Reliant a Giant'. The tragedy of the decision to pursue a discarded Italian design, based on an entirely new chassis made in Germany and powered by bought-in engines and running gear, is now far more evident with hindsight.

Much earlier on Reliant did have a stab at producing a rather radical four-wheeled sports car, using their own alloy engine, which was known as the FW7. This involved a rear-engine design with its own specific chassis and transmission, which would have been a huge project for a major manufacturer let alone little Reliant and it is not surprising it did not materialise. Ogle were involved in the body design of this radical two-seater and persisted in their ideas for a Reliant-based product to fill a niche in the small sports car or leisure market. Hence the appearance of the remarkable Bond Bug. Despite the name incorporating the newly acquired Bond Company, the Bug was entirely based on the Reliant three-wheeler chassis and engine. It was a most exciting and brave development, promoted by Ray Wiggin in characteristic fashion and was even exhibited at the Design Centre and proved to be a good seller, albeit not a profitable one. With development it could still be on sale today, I suspect, as an alternative to the extraordinary two-seater town cars that seem to be appearing from all quarters of the world. In fact the recent management of Reliant did play with the idea of re-introducing the Bond Bug in four-wheeled form, after such a vehicle was produced privately by Hampshire-based Mike Webster, but this came to nothing.

The core of all these projects is the stalwart alloy engine produced by Reliant since before the Second World War in various capacities from 600cc to the present OHV 850cc form. As such it has been the lifeblood of 750 Motor Club activities in racing and trials. This club started in motor sport using the venerable Austin 7 750cc engine. It is well known that the Reliant engine is based on that Austin engine and that it has been further developed over the years. Even a twin-cam version was created, producing considerable power for its size. It was considered too powerful for a three-wheeler but would have been ideal for sports-car application had such a car been developed by Reliant. Also Reliant feared that the traditional three-wheeler owner would not have appreciated the additional complication of a twin-cam engine after the simple to maintain OHV unit.

More recently, a privately built special, based on the Reliant Rebel of the 1970s, has been used in trials and once again this car demonstrates the potential for a cheap sporting car, which could have feasibly been made by Reliant. The home-built design closely follows the Lotus 7 shape which has proved to be timeless and regularly copied with great success by such firms as Westfield, who sell their high-powered version for five-figure sums. However, there is almost certainly a market for a similar car with less power and fuel thirst costing below £10,000. There seem few reasons why Reliant could not produce such a car within this budget considering the prices of their existing cars. They still have all the tooling to produce a four-wheeled chassis since the last vehicle so equipped, the Fox pick-up, was made as recently as 1984. Furthermore, a two-seater sports car would require far less material, including fibreglass bodywork, fittings, upholstery and glass which are fundamental when costing production.

These apparent lost opportunities are due to the absence of the brave and inspired management personified by Ray Wiggin, who was truly the 'Father of Reliant Sports Cars', and his like has been sorely missed for the last twenty years. As recently as 1995 another sports coupé was promised by Reliant when they were under the ownership of Beans. Visitors to the Motor Show were greeted by a stand with an empty space and a drawing on the wall and it seems likely that the vacant space symbolises the slim prospects of another Reliant-built sports car ever being produced.

This 750 Formula trophy for national racing championships run by the 750 Motor Club is a fitting symbol of the success and respect the sporting fraternity had for the sturdy Reliant alloy engine. The projects seen on the following pages are entirely dependent on this long-lived unit.

In 1976 Tony Stevens, an independent designer, recognised the gap in the sports-car market left by the decline of small production cars such as the Spridget and Spitfire. For economic reasons a vehicle to fill this gap needed to be based on an existing platform, preferably with a separate chassis. The Reliant Kitten fitted this requirement and was the basis of his Sienna two-seater, seen here.

The bodyshape was reminiscent of the Arkley conversion for Austin-Healey Sprites when the bodywork had become too rotten. The traditional shape had served Morgan very well and was economical to produce in metal or fibreglass and would have been extremely simple for Reliant to produce as they had all the running gear in production at the time.

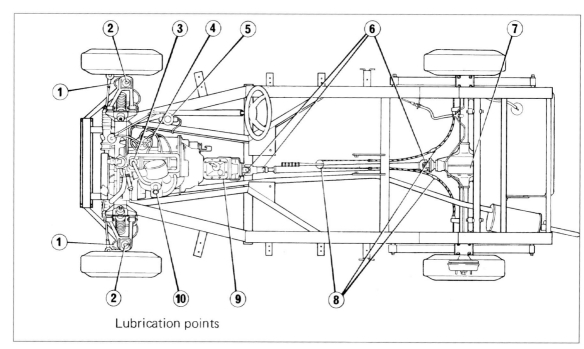

Lubrication points

This outline of the Reliant Kitten chassis shows what a substantial design it was for such a small car and thus ideal for an open sports car of the type Tony Stevens planned. The light alloy engine and gearbox situated well behind the front axle line and the rack and pinion steering offered the prospect of excellent handling.

Tony Stevens is seen here seated on the front of the one and only Sienna (still in the family's possession in Warwick), and seems to be exuding all the frustration he must have felt at the lack of response from Reliant or any other backer for his project. The car looked professionally built and with the exception of the radiator grille was most attractive.

Undeterred, Tony Stevens again returned to the Reliant Kitten chassis for his next proposal, the Cipher. This was intended to be a far more sophisticated car and involved rather more modification to the original chassis in order to achieve the required low build and handling qualities. The bare chassis is seen here and it is hard to detect which part of it is still from the donor model. It was, however, a very sound design and eminently viable for a firm such as Reliant to build.

The bodywork designed by Stevens for the Cipher was immensely attractive and vaguely reminiscent of the successful Lotus Elan. Moulds were made and the idea was presented to Ritchie Spencer, Managing Director of Reliant at the time, with a view to production. Certainly the appearance of the Cipher must have proved attractive to Reliant as they agreed to assemble one as a pilot operation.

One of two Cipher prototypes being assembled in the Reliant development department. However, the management came to the conclusion that the Cipher would be too costly to engineer into a production car, possibly because of the alterations to the Kitten chassis. Certainly the body moulding would not have proved expensive to produce with their experience in this field and mechanically it used all existing Reliant running gear. The alternative decision to adopt a Michelotti design fitted to a brand-new style of chassis propelled by Ford running gear defies understanding. Sadly, that decision was to spell the premature end to Reliant sports cars and result in many financial losses for the company.

The Cipher shape responded well to this two-tone colour scheme and there is little doubt that it would have been a sales success at the right price. *Motor* magazine gave the prototype a glowing report when they tested it in April 1981 when it was fitted with the 848cc Reliant engine in standard tune. They achieved a maximum speed of 93mph and a 0–60mph time of 17 seconds. Allied to an overall economy of 44mpg, these figures far exceed those of the 948cc engined Frogeyed Sprite, to which the Cipher was invariably compared.

Though disheartened by Reliant's rejection of the Cipher, Tony Stevens proceeded to build six examples in all. The number of separate body mouldings used are seen here in his workshop. Undoubtedly, Reliant could have reduced this number of individual mouldings for production purposes, but the original design did lend itself to low-cost moulds and ease of repair by having bolt-on sections. This alone should have persuaded Reliant to adopt this design instead of the ill-fated SS1, about which the press and public were very dubious from the outset. Most of the Ciphers still exist and have proved very durable and economic to run, emphasising the tragedy of the opportunity missed by Reliant.

After the successful launch of the GTE, in 1969, Tom Karen of Ogle Design proposed an advanced wedge-shaped sports car concept based on a mid-engined format to be allied to a backbone chassis designed by John Crosthwaite. This design anticipated the Triumph TR7, penned by Harris Mann and revealed in 1975, which indicates how advanced Ogle's thinking was at that time. The retractable headlights were also very modern, although the Lamborghini Muira did have unconcealed versions in 1966.

This revolutionary concept was termed FW7 (FW standing for four-wheeled) and was powered by a twin-carburettor version of the current 850cc Reliant engine. This was mounted behind the driver with the in-line gearbox ahead of it, transmitting the drive by Hi-Vo chain down to a propshaft connected to the live rear axle. This was located by radius arms and an 'A' bracket for lateral control.

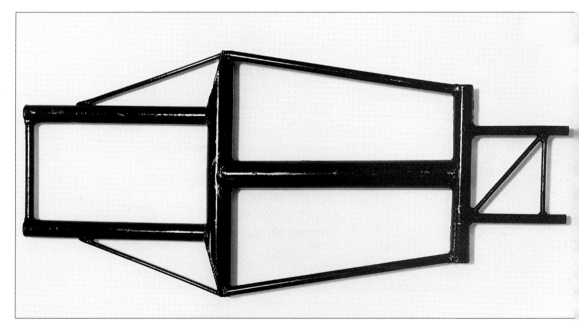

The tubular chassis destined for the doomed FW7 project was delightfully simple yet sturdy. It featured a strong central backbone and rear section (left) to support the rear engine. The full triangulation would have resulted in a very rigid base for this exciting project which could not be produced, so far ahead of its time, for financial reasons.

The light weight of the Reliant all-alloy engine is dramatically demonstrated by this display of strength by a Reliant manager carrying the complete engine without undue strain. Such lightness was imperative to Reliant as their three-wheelers had to weigh under 8cwt complete to run, in order to qualify for a motorcycle licence, which was their main attraction to loyal customers.

Reliant had one main competitor in the three-wheeler market and that was Bond Cars of Preston. In 1969 Reliant made a successful bid for Bond with a view to removing the competition and gaining access to Triumph dealers, since Bond made Triumph-based Equipe models. The first new model from the combined operation was a rather surprising Ogle-designed leisure vehicle called the Bond Bug. Built around the established Reliant Regal chassis and powered by the current 700cc all-alloy engine, this wedge-shaped car without conventional doors but with a lift-up front canopy was indeed a brave move.

Priced at about £550, it was clearly aimed at the young driver of seventeen to twenty-five years old and it had no real competition but took on the task of establishing a trend for a fun vehicle that was both practical and economic and above all stylish. Reliant aimed at producing 2,000 Bugs a year but never reached this level of sales in the short period it was in production. It could be driven on a motorcycle licence, as all the three-wheelers could be, and it offered a speed in excess of 70mph, as well as 70mpg at a constant 40mph. Also, Reliant offered a two-year warranty at least twenty years before the larger manufacturers considered such a move.

Tom Karen of Ogle Design admitted that he had been dreaming of this type of vehicle for twenty years and now that he was working with such a courageous leader of Reliant in the person of Ray Wiggin he was able to realise this ambition. Clever features, apart from the lift-up canopy, were seats that were moulded into the main bodyshell. The stout construction of the chassis with the engine between the passengers made it quite a safe vehicle during frontal impact. The centre of gravity was also very low and biased to the rear making it far more stable than the average three-wheeler.

The dimensions of the Bond Bug were advantageous when parking as this amusing arrangement illustrates. The Hodge Group, who owned Reliant at the time, also offered favourable insurance rates of £25 per annum for young drivers, how times have changed! Amusingly, the Bug was only offered in one colour, bright orange, which became known as 'Bug Tangerine'. The Bug was possibly ahead of its time as a town car and proved very expensive to manufacture.

One private development of a Reliant Rebel four-wheeler into a trials special was constructed in 1997 by Iain Daniels from Stroud, in the midst of favourite trials country. The chassis and suspension are standard Rebel items, apart from the rear axle location by radius arms, panhard rod and coil springs as on the Bond Bug. The bodywork was hand-formed aluminium sheet over a tubular framework welded to the original Rebel chassis. Separate motor-cycle wings cover the wheels and the whole car is registered and often driven to trials meetings where it is achieving notable success against more sophisticated machines.

Although following similar principles to Stevens' Sienna, this Rebel-based two-seater is far more in tune with the present trend in sporting two-seaters and could very easily be considered a junior Caterham 7. With suitable refinements and bodywork moulded in fibreglass it surely would be capable of being produced by Reliant as they have all the tooling to produce the chassis, and the running gear is still in production.

This front shot of the Daniels' Rebel special shows the high setting of the front suspension for trials work, where extreme ground clearance is necessary. However, it would be very simple to lower the suspension front and rear by using shorter spring/damper units for extended road use, where a low centre of gravity is more desirable.

This driver's eye view illustrates the standard Rebel instrument binnacle and gear-lever position, both ideally placed. The well-braced body structure, welded to the original Rebel chassis, can also be seen. Without the need for doors, the whole car is very rigid and surely would be even cheaper to manufacture than the corresponding saloon since the amount of materials utilised is much less.

The 750 Motor Club evolved around a competition car built on the basis of the venerable pre-war Austin 7, which had a 747cc engine. Since Reliant adopted this engine for their early three-wheeled cars and carried on producing it there was a natural bond between Reliant and the 750 MC, which depended on the continued availability of the engine and spares for it. Eventually, Reliant designed their own OHV all-alloy engine based on the Austin 7 design and this engine was approved by the 750 MC for their race cars, one of which is seen here.

Another favourite application of the 750cc Reliant engine was in trials specials of the sort seen here. Its light weight and reliability, allied to the slick Reliant gearbox, were valued features in this

sport. Some specials also used the rear axle produced by Reliant for their economy cars, so in many ways they could be considered Reliant sports cars.

INDEX

—